Once upon a CAMPUS

Tantalizing Truths about College from People Who've Already Messed Up

Edited by Supurna Banerjee

KAPLAN

Published by Simon & Schuster

New York   London   Toronto   Sydney

Kaplan Publishing
Published by Simon & Schuster, Inc.
1230 Avenue of the Americas
New York, NY 10020

For bulk sales to schools, colleges, and universities, please contact: Order Department, Simon & Schuster, Inc., 100 Front Street, Riverside, NJ 08075. Phone: (800) 223-2336. Fax: (800) 943-9831.

For information regarding special discounts for other bulk purchases, please contact Simon & Schuster Special Sales at 1-800-456-6798 or business@simonandschuster.com

Cover Design: Bradford Foltz
Cover Illustration: Kim Johnson
Interior Design: Lisa Stokes, Lili Schwartz
Editor: Beth Grupper

Manufactured in the United States of America

May 2005
10 9 8 7 6 5 4 3 2 1

Library of Congress Cataloging-in-Publication Data
ISBN 0-7432-5185-7

ACKNOWLEDGMENTS

I would like to thank my family and my friends, for all the support in the form of long-distance phone calls that I received while working on this project. A special thank you to my roommate, Karen, for her help on getting that first difficult chapter finished. Finally, my sincere thanks to Maureen McMahon for giving me my first job opportunity out of college.

–Supurna Banerjee

The publisher would like to thank Colin Shields for his contribution to this project.

TABLE OF CONTENTS

So you're off to college for the first time. Nervous? Sure, there will be new classes, new friends, new professors, a new living situation, and a whole new way of life to contend with—but that's the exciting part! Okay, so you're still nervous. Don't worry. This book is here to help.

Packed with advice from students and recent grads across the country, ONCE UPON A CAMPUS will show you how to make college fun, rewarding, and memorable. These students have lived through it themselves, and now you get to benefit from their wisdom—and learn from their mistakes.

These pages hold tales from the tormented, funny stories and solutions, and the secrets to surviving your freshman year and beyond. Want the inside scoop on how to survive—and thrive—from day one? Then start reading!

WELCOME TO COLLEGE

Don't expect to recognize yourself four years from now.

GRADUATE, ENGLISH/PSYCHOLOGY, VASSAR COLLEGE

I thought I was the only one who was nervous, but as it turns out, **everyone** felt exactly the same way I did!

SOPHOMORE, BIOLOGY, BOSTON COLLEGE

I assumed that everyone was much smarter than I was, but eventually I realized that ALL STUDENTS STRUGGLE in some way—I wasn't alone.

GRADUATE, ENGLISH, PRINCETON UNIVERSITY

It seemed like everyone was really nice. Slowly, I found out who really was a nice person...
and who wasn't. **Be careful** who you trust at first!

GRADUATE, PSYCHOLOGY, MUHLENBERG COLLEGE

I noticed that people of the same background tended to stick together. Unfortunately, this was the way it was throughout college. **I wish** people had branched out more.

JUNIOR, PHARMACOLOGY, UNIVERSITY OF CONNECTICUT

At first I felt lost at my huge university, but it turned out to be a smaller community than I expected.

SENIOR, ENGLISH, RUTGERS UNIVERSITY

I thought professors were these scary, unapproachable people. Turns out MOST PROFESSORS ARE HAPPY TO HELP students achieve their best.

SENIOR, PHYSICAL THERAPY, ITHACA COLLEGE

FRESHMAN ORIENTATION

At orientation **everything is thrown at you at once** and it feels very overwhelming, but you are not asked to know everything right away. Just know that they are exposing you to as many things as possible to get you excited about the school.

GRADUATE, BIOLOGY, UNIVERSITY OF CENTRAL FLORIDA

It's a real paradox, the orientation experience, because although it was miserable and seemed pointless, it definitely made **a lasting impact**—and being in a new place where I didn't know a single person, those ridiculous "getting-to-know-you" games helped me make some connections with people. I needed to know that I wasn't alone.

GRADUATE, ART AND DESIGN, LAGRANGE COLLEGE

An ironing board. You think you won't use it, but it comes in handy when you want to wear a shirt you just pulled from a pile of clothes on your floor.

SOPHOMORE, BIOLOGICAL SCIENCES, RUTGERS UNIVERSITY

Envelopes and stamps. Email is easier, but there's nothing better than going to your mailbox and seeing it full of letters from your favorite people!

JUNIOR, ECONOMICS, UNION COLLEGE

A mini sewing kit. You have no idea how many times you will need it.

SOPHOMORE, WRITING, BOSTON COLLEGE

An open mind—there are so many new things to experience!

GRADUATE, CHEMICAL ENGINEERING, UNIVERSITY OF RHODE ISLAND

ONE THING I COULDN'T HAVE MADE IT THROUGH COLLEGE WITHOUT WAS...

Febreze. Instant washing machine.

SENIOR, GERMAN/PSYCHOLOGY, UNIVERSITY OF FLORIDA

A hot plate. You can literally cook anything on it and it fits in your crowded dorm room.

SENIOR, ENGLISH, FORDHAM UNIVERSITY

Pictures of family and friends. It dofinitely helps when you're feeling homesick!

JUNIOR, PHOTOGRAPHY, ROCHESTER INSTITUTE OF TECHNOLOGY

My 5-subject notebook—it's much easier than carrying multiple notebooks and you never grab the wrong one.

GRADUATE, LEGAL STUDIES, UNIVERSITY OF MASSACHUSETTS—AMHERST

Extra pajamas. They became my staple after my second week.

GRADUATE, ECONOMICS, CORNELL UNIVERSITY

RAMEN NOODLES and Coca-Cola!!!

GRADUATE, SPEECH-LANGUAGE PATHOLOGY, TOWSON UNIVERSITY

2

FREE AT LAST . . . NOW WHAT?

Freedom is like a gallon of ice cream—you can overdo it and eat the entire thing at once, but you'll be pretty sick of it afterwards.

SENIOR, POLITICAL SCIENCE/CHINESE LANGUAGE,
UNIVERSITY OF CALIFORNIA—IRVINE

I could do what I wanted when I wanted. It didn't matter if I felt like going to get a Slurpee from 7-Eleven at 3 a.m. I didn't have to ask permission. It was great!

SENIOR, BIOLOGY, MARY WASHINGTON COLLEGE

I WENT A LITTLE CRAZY and got a rock star boyfriend who turned out to be trouble, but a good distraction. It is really tough to manage independence for the first time, but the school I went to offered free counseling and it was amazingly helpful.

SENIOR, JOURNALISM, UNIVERSITY OF TEXAS—AUSTIN

I drank a beer, got a belly-button ring, and just before Christmas break my freshman year, I got a tattoo. I still drink beer, lost the belly-button ring, and fortunately, my tattoo is in a very inconspicuous place. My political career will be safe.

GRADUATE, POLITICAL SCIENCE/ENGLISH, VIRGINIA POLYTECHNIC INSTITUTE AND STATE UNIVERSITY

Freedom is great until you need your family. I took off, went out all the time, never called home. But when you get sick, stressed out, or nervous and you need a comforting word, it's nice to have that connection.

SENIOR, NEUROSCIENCE, UNIVERSITY OF ROCHESTER

It was great to get away from home. The sense of freedom and doing whatever you want helps you mature faster, I think, because your parents aren't there to push you. You just have to DO WHAT YOU FEEL IS THE RIGHT THING to do.

SENIOR, PRE-LAW/MASS COMMUNICATIONS, OHIO STATE UNIVERSITY

I did everything my parents told me not to do, made up my own mind about what I thought was right and wrong, and eventually **came to the same conclusions** as my parents. Funny, isn't it?

GRADUATE, BIOLOGY, COLLEGE OF CHARLESTON

ONCE UPON A CAMPUS

I WENT CRAZY the first semester of college. I didn't do well at all, especially since I was taking Chemistry and Trigonometry. It's really easy to get caught up in the partying. Don't let it get in the way of what you're in college for.

GRADUATE, ENGLISH, UNIVERSITY OF FLORIDA

At first I definitely went a little crazy, but **after a while I realized** what I needed to do and I did it. Unfortunately, my freshman grades are what will probably keep me out of a great graduate school.

SENIOR, ACCOUNTING, UTAH STATE UNIVERSITY

A little craziness never hurt anybody—unless you go down-right wild. Have fun, do things you've never done before, go to parties (you don't have to drink), go on dates. I personally loved "going out." You can't stay up till 2 a.m. forever, so enjoy it while it lasts!

GRADUATE, MASS COMMUNICATIONS, NORTHEASTERN STATE

ONCE UPON A CAMPUS

13

I explored my surroundings. I spent time by myself during the day because I could. College is one of the only times in your life where you can spend three hours during the day reading in a coffee shop or at the student lounge.

SENIOR, ANTHROPOLOGY, UNIVERSITY OF TORONTO

I drove for miles on the slightest whim. My friends and I drove to the Oregon coast, a two-hour drive, at 4 a.m. so we could greet the sunrise; we drove to Seattle, a four-hour drive, so we could go to a concert on a Friday night; WE TRAVELED EVERYWHERE AND DIDN'T EVER SLEEP.

GRADUATE, BIOCHEMISTRY/MOLECULAR BIOLOGY, REED COLLEGE

EVERYTHING IN MODERATION

When I was a freshman I used to stay out until all hours of the night (and early morning) not really doing much of anything. My friends and I made 3 a.m. runs to Denny's and Steak n' Shake. But I made sure that if I did those spur of the moment things, **I stayed up and did homework** the next night.

SENIOR, BIOLOGY, OBERLIN COLLEGE

Exercise your newfound freedom moderately. **Don't overdo it;** because your opportunity to attend college can easily be taken away if you fail academically.

SENIOR, CHINESE LANGUAGE, UNIVERSITY OF CALIFORNIA—IRVINE

Independence isn't all it's cracked up to be once the bills start rolling in.

GRADUATE, POLITICAL SCIENCE, UNIVERSITY OF COLORADO—DENVER

The college experience helps MERGE YOUNG ADULTS INTO THE REAL WORLD. During my freshman year in college I was faced with paying numerous bills, balancing my checkbook, doing my own laundry, and cooking and cleaning.

SENIOR, PSYCHOLOGY/CRIMINOLOGY, FLORIDA STATE UNIVERSITY

I actually matured faster. Once I had **the freedom I had been longing for,** I found out that there really was not much that I wanted to do that I had not been able to do before.

GRADUATE, ECONOMICS, UNIVERSITY OF ALABAMA—TUSCALOOSA

3

YOU'RE NOT IN HIGH SCHOOL ANYMORE

If you flew through your classes in high school . . . brace yourself. College is a whole new world!

SENIOR, BIOLOGY/CHEMISTRY, DENISON UNIVERSITY

THE DIFFERENCE IS CLEAR

You can cram and slide your way through high school, but it is difficult to do that—and do well—in college. Force yourself to **be disciplined and diligent.** It will pay off.

GRADUATE, ENGLISH/FRENCH, CORNELL UNIVERSITY

High school is nothing like college. You actually have to **make an effort** in college.

GRADUATE, BIOLOGY, CLEMSON UNIVERSITY

You will spend a lot more time DOING HOMEWORK in college. Many teachers believe that their class is your only class.

GRADUATE, PSYCHOLOGY/BIOLOGY, SAINT LOUIS UNIVERSITY

There is no formula for success. During freshman year a lot of time is spent finding out about yourself along with expanding your academic capabilities.

SENIOR, GENDER STUDIES/RELIGIOUS STUDIES, BROWN UNIVERSITY

High school teachers teach you everything you need to know. College professors assume you're going to TEACH YOURSELF.

GRADUATE, CHEMICAL ENGINEERING, UNIVERSITY OF VIRGINIA

For the first time in your life it's YOUR responsibility to make sure your work gets done. Mom and Dad aren't there to watch over your shoulder. **If you don't do your work, you'll fail**—so do it for yourself. Anyway, it feels better doing it for yourself than for your parents.

GRADUATE, BIOMETRY AND STATISTICS, CORNELL UNIVERSITY

What most people don't realize is that you don't learn from the books you are reading, you learn from the APPLICATION OF THAT KNOWLEDGE. High school tests often quiz memorization skills. That's a handy talent to have, but unless you can apply what you are learning, the whole process is a waste.

GRADUATE, POLITICAL SCIENCE, ST. JOSEPH'S UNIVERSITY

Know the syllabus backward and forward so that you know **when you need to focus** hard on school and when you can relax.

SENIOR, HUMAN DEVELOPMENT AND FAMILY STUDIES, TEXAS TECH UNIVERSITY

A lot of people get through high school without doing much work. If you've taken AP courses or some accelerated courses be glad you did, because those help. There is a lot more **independent work** involved with college. If you can study independently and learn from a book, you will have a great advantage.

GRADUATE, MATH, CARLETON COLLEGE

JUST MORE OF THE SAME

College is not more difficult than high school, except that now you are battling **a thousand distractions.**

GRADUATE, PSYCHOLOGY, NEW YORK UNIVERSITY

If you were truly doing what you were supposed to do in high school, college academics aren't that different. Just remember that there usually isn't a homework score to bring your average up, but **every class** is designed so that you can bomb one test and still get an "A."

GRADUATE, POLITICAL SCIENCE, COLORADO STATE UNIVERSITY

The core curriculum in college is really designed to help you make a smooth transition from high school. However, just like the transition from junior high to high school, you have to get into a groove. Until you do, look for support from other students, perhaps sophomores and juniors, and don't be afraid to ask for help.

GRADUATE, PSYCHOLOGY, COLBY-SAWYER COLLEGE

HOW TO SURVIVE
THE DORM

*Realize that if you can make it through
one year in the smallest room ever, you will
appreciate every other place you live for the
rest of your life.*

SENIOR, MARKETING, UNIVERSITY OF NOTRE DAME

ROLL WITH THE PUNCHES

Be flexible. People will be loud, annoying, irritating—just GO WITH THE FLOW and try not to let your feathers get ruffled.

SENIOR, NEUROSCIENCE, UNIVERSITY OF ROCHESTER

Realize that everyone in the dorm makes sacrifices to **live together**. Don't get bent out of shape about the little things—talk things out calmly and don't hold grudges.

GRADUATE, ART AND DESIGN, LAGRANGE COLLEGE

Don't sweat the small stuff... if you sweat those things profusely, you'll go nuts (and probably dehydrate).

SENIOR, GENETICS, IOWA STATE UNIVERSITY

Find someplace you can call your own. Suddenly you are living with a bunch of kids your age, none of who really know you. It can be overwhelming. Putting aside personal time and space becomes really important to your happiness.

GRADUATE, ENGLISH/FRENCH, CORNELL UNIVERSITY

Be open and talk to your hall mates. Suppressing inhibitions and fears of talking to the "stranger next door" is key to adjusting to dorm life, particularly when homesickness rears its head.

GRADUATE, SOCIOLOGY/POLITICAL SCIENCE, STATE UNIVERSITY OF NEW YORK—BUFFALO

MAKE FRIENDS ON YOUR HALL. If you do, you will always be guaranteed to have someone to go to dinner with and possibly find a new roommate for next year.

GRADUATE, BIOLOGY AND NUTRITION, PENNSYLVANIA STATE UNIVERSITY

Have friends outside your dorm. Dorms, by the second month of school, tend to turn into soap operas. You need a place where you can go **HANG OUT WITH FRIENDS WHO DON'T LIVE WITH YOU**.

GRADUATE, POLITICAL SCIENCE, ST. JOSEPH'S UNIVERSITY

Make friends inside the hall, but **get involved** in clubs so you are out and about a lot, and coming home feels like home—not a prison where you spend all your time.

GRADUATE, SOCIOLOGY/FAMILY STUDIES AND HUMAN DEVELOPMENT, UNIVERSITY OF ARIZONA

Stay away from "hall-cest" (hooking up with/dating someone in the same hall or dorm as you) if your hall is small. You will feel like you are married, because that person is ALWAYS THERE!!!! And it will be BAD if you break up in the middle of the year, 'cause you will see the person ALL THE TIME!!!

SENIOR, BIOLOGY, OBERLIN COLLEGE

Remember that the people on your hall DON'T have to be your best friends. If you make your circle of friends out of only your dorm buddies, a disagreement within your hall can not only make your living situation hard, it can also mess with your social life. It's best to **have friends from numerous places,** like from your activities and classes, rather than from just your hall.

GRADUATE, ENGLISH/MUSIC, THE COLLEGE OF WILLIAM & MARY

Some dorms prescreen people with similar interests. If there's **a hobby or lifestyle** that you feel passionate about, see if your college has this option.

SENIOR, PHILOSOPHY, ITHACA COLLEGE

DON'T BE A DOORMAT. If people are being too loud in the dorms, talk to your RA, buy earplugs . . . do something. Don't assume that you have to just take it because you live there.

JUNIOR, CREATIVE WRITING, OBERLIN COLLEGE

ONCE UPON A CAMPUS

Wash your hands often. Although it sounds silly, it will help you stay healthy when others around you get sick.

GRADUATE, HEALTH AND SOCIETY, UNIVERSITY OF ROCHESTER

WEAR FLIP-FLOPS in the shower. You don't want what grows in the shower to grow on your feet!

SENIOR, ENVIRONMENTAL DESIGN, TEXAS A&M UNIVERSITY—COLLEGE STATION

Think with your head when it comes to **your health** and your belongings. Get hepatitis B and meningitis vaccinations.

GRADUATE, HISTORY, RUTGERS UNIVERSITY

YOU'LL USE DUCT TAPE FOR EVERYTHING. Anything you need to hold together, from your car to your backpack to your room, duct tape will fix much more cheaply than any alternative!

GRADUATE, PSYCHOLOGY, XAVIER UNIVERSITY

The keys to surviving dorm life: patience, headphones, earplugs, and a bottle of echinacea/Vitamin C.

GRADUATE, EARLY CHILDHOOD AND ELEMENTARY EDUCATION, NEW YORK UNIVERSITY

Have **enough underwear** to last the whole term, just in case you don't get around to doing laundry.

GRADUATE, GOVERNMENT, DARTMOUTH COLLEGE

Downy Wrinkle Releaser and Shout® Wipes are key. You'll never have to IRON OR WASH again if you don't want to.

GRADUATE, ECONOMICS, UNIVERSITY OF ALABAMA—TUSCALOOSA

Stock up on socks. The more socks you have, the less laundry you'll have to do.

GRADUATE, ENGINEERING SCIENCES, DARTMOUTH COLLEGE

Quarters become a precious commodity when you go away to college. Don't think you can put dollars in those washing machines.

GRADUATE, HISTORY, UNIVERSITY OF MASSACHUSETTS

DON'T DO LAUNDRY ON WEEKENDS. It will take you forever to finish, because chances are everyone will be doing laundry then and you won't be able to use more than one machine at a time.

GRADUATE, ENGLISH, PRINCETON UNIVERSITY

When I got to college my freshman year I didn't know how to do my own laundry. I spent a month washing my clothes in fabric softener. What did I know?

SENIOR, ENGLISH/CREATIVE WRITING AND FILM/PHOTOGRAPHY, HOLLINS UNIVERSITY

Don't leave your laundry sitting in the machines for hours. People WILL take your wet clothes out of the washers and leave them on the floor.

SENIOR, ENGLISH, FORDHAM UNIVERSITY

DORM ESSENTIALS

Pack a fan. Dorm rooms are stifling!

GRADUATE, PSYCHOLOGY, UNIVERSITY OF ALABAMA—TUSCALOOSA

A backrest for reading in bed makes studying more comfortable.

SENIOR, ANTHROPOLOGY, UNIVERSITY OF TORONTO

A toolbox—you never know when you'll need a hammer or a screwdriver.

SENIOR, INTERNATIONAL BUSINESS, XAVIER UNIVERSITY

Many **RETAIL STORES AND WEBSITES** have special college sections (some are only up during back-to-school season, others are up year round) to help students shop for essential college supplies. Check out www.bedbathandbeyond.com.

SENIOR, GOVERNMENT, DARTMOUTH COLLEGE

THE ROOMMATE FACTOR

I had a single (thank God).

GRADUATE, PSYCHOLOGY, UNIVERSITY OF
CALIFORNIA –SAN DIEGO

Remember the #1 rule: **if it would annoy you** if your roommate did it, it will probably annoy your roommate if you do it.

GRADUATE, CHEMICAL ENGINEERING, UNIVERSITY OF VIRGINIA

HAVE EARPLUGS AND AN EYE-MASK so you can sleep at night, even when your roommate isn't.

GRADUATE, ENVIRONMENTAL STUDIES, EMORY & HENRY COLLEGE

All roommates are weird. The key is realizing that **your roommate is weird (and so are you)** and deciding to get along with her anyway.

SENIOR, BIOLOGY, SEATTLE PACIFIC UNIVERSITY

Be extra tolerant and just remember that the other person is going through some of the same things that you are—and they may never have had to share a room before.

SENIOR, EDUCATION, UNIVERSITY OF CALIFORNIA—SANTA CRUZ

Have an open mind. Unless your roommate is disrespectful, you have to realize that EVERYBODY IS DIFFERENT and be willing to adjust to those differences.

JUNIOR, BIOLOGY, OHIO STATE UNIVERSITY

A good roommate should never disrespect you, your things, or your opinions.

GRADUATE, PRE-MEDICINE, PENNSYLVANIA STATE UNIVERSITY

Don't assume that what works for you will work for your roommate. As you will quickly learn, people come to college from all different kinds of backgrounds. Whether it's walking around the room naked or using his stuff without permission, he may feel differently than you about various issues. **Always ask first.**

GRADUATE, NEUROSCIENCE AND BEHAVIOR, WESLEYAN UNIVERSITY

A STRANGER IS THE WAY TO GO

I roomed with a girl I knew from home for the first two years of college. It greatly hindered me from getting to know new people. **Don't room with someone you already know!**

GRADUATE, BIOLOGY, SAINT JOSEPH'S UNIVERSITY

Living with your good friends is not always the best option. You'll learn things about them that **YOU'LL WISH YOU HADN'T**, and you might not end up being friends afterward.

SENIOR, PSYCHOLOGY, UNIVERSITY OF ILLINOIS—URBANA-CHAMPAIGN

NEVER try to "mother" your roommate. I had a roommate who would try to regulate my naps and my schedule—it drove me crazy!

GRADUATE, CRIMINAL JUSTICE, VITERBO UNIVERSITY

BE WILLING TO COMPROMISE with your roommate. If she wants to have her boyfriend over and you can't stand him, talk to her about it and figure out a solution.

SENIOR, BIOMEDICAL SCIENCES, MARQUETTE UNIVERSITY

If you arrive at college before your roommate, do not choose your bed, drawers, or closet. **Wait until your roommate arrives** and then draw straws or flip a coin. You never want to seem inconsiderate on Day One.

GRADUATE, ENGLISH/FRENCH, CORNELL UNIVERSITY

Respect people's spaces. If you're a little more reserved at first until you're comfortable with each other, you'll probably be better off.

SENIOR, EDUCATION, STATE UNIVERSITY OF NEW YORK—ALBANY

No roommate should ever interfere with her roommate's sleeping pattern. This includes: never slamming the door when your roommate is sleeping, trying to keep the lights off as much as possible when you have to stay up late or wake up early, and discussing whether sleeping with the TV or radio on is okay with her.

GRADUATE, ENGLISH, TEXAS WOMEN'S UNIVERSITY

A GOOD ROOMMATE should never assume that he knows what you are thinking. Communication is vital in such a small space.

GRADUATE, HISTORY, UNIVERSITY OF MASSACHUSETTS

Don't hold a grudge. Little arguments can quickly become catastrophes when confined to closed spaces. **Learn to forgive quickly.**

GRADUATE, BIOCHEMISTRY, UNIVERSITY OF CALIFORNIA—DAVIS

ONCE UPON A CAMPUS

Learn to speak up for yourself. Even if your roommates are wonderful, there are bound to be confrontations, and the only way to solve them is by learning to say what needs to be said in a constructive way.

SENIOR, PHILOSOPHY, STATE UNIVERSITY OF NEW YORK—ALBANY

Check out the official procedures at your school for **DEALING WITH ROOMMATE CONFLICTS.** If things are really bad, most schools have a process by which you can try to swap out roommates or move.

JUNIOR, BIOLOGY, JOHNS HOPKINS UNIVERSITY

A good roommate would never put her roommate in danger. I had a roommate who would bring men into the bedroom, completely intoxicated. She would leave them there and go back out. So I would wake up to some drunken stranger in my room.

GRADUATE, ECONOMICS, NEW YORK UNIVERSITY

A GOOD ROOMMATE should never leave defrosting sheep hearts in the fridge uncovered, so they drip on your cans of Mountain Dew.

GRADUATE, BIOCHEMISTRY/CELL BIOLOGY, UNIVERSITY OF CALIFORNIA—SAN DIEGO

A good roommate should never use his roommate's dish scrubber to clean a neighbor's bathroom floor for money.

SENIOR, PSYCHOLOGY, ARIZONA STATE UNIVERSITY

ONCE UPON A CAMPUS

47

My roommates were always there to support me. It meant a lot that I could always turn to them.

GRADUATE, THEATER, DREW UNIVERSITY

My roommate brought me out of my shell so much. She made a huge impact on my life and has changed the way I think about so many things. **I was lucky** to have been assigned to her.

SENIOR, PSYCHOLOGY, BARNARD COLLEGE

My roommate was there for **advice without judgment** when it was desperately needed.

SENIOR, ENGLISH, VILLANOVA UNIVERSITY

My roommate gave me the confidence to try things at college I had never done before. It was great to know that **he was a great friend** who was always watching my back.

GRADUATE, ENGINEERING, RENSSELAER POLYTECHNIC INSTITUTE

TIME MANAGEMENT

It's going to seem like you have a lot of free time because you are only in class for three to four hours a day. When midterms come around, however, you will realize what you were supposed to be doing during that "free time."

GRADUATE, BIOLOGY, COLLEGE OF CHARLESTON

To keep up with your reading, JUST READ, READ, READ, AND DON'T STOP. . . .

SENIOR, PSYCHOLOGY, STATE UNIVERSITY OF NEW YORK—BUFFALO

Keep up with your work from the beginning. Study EVERY night.

GRADUATE, POLITICAL SCIENCE, LOUISIANA STATE UNIVERSITY

Don't let things slide—you can't make up an entire semester's worth of work the night before a final.

SENIOR, JOURNALISM/PHILOSOPHY, SYRACUSE UNIVERSITY

It sounds like a lot of work, but it really is important to **study at least a little bit every day.** If you study for a hard class every day, you won't need to cram for a test and you will have a much better understanding of the class material.

SENIOR, BIOMEDICAL SCIENCES, MARQUETTE UNIVERSITY

Stay up to date in every class and learn the material from the day's lecture that night. Then the prep time before a test will be all review. That is the secret.

GRADUATE, BIOLOGY/ENGLISH, SPRING HILL COLLEGE

You cannot leave anything till the last minute. For tests, begin reviewing a few days in advance. For papers, the amount of time depends on the length of the paper, but leave yourself enough time to do a good outline, rough draft, and final version.

GRADUATE, GOVERNMENT, DARTMOUTH COLLEGE

Figure out what works best for you in terms of time management. Do you write better under pressure or do you like to have a lot of time to revise? Do you want to talk to professors to get advice? **Learn to manage your time, basically.**

GRADUATE, ANTHROPOLOGY/INTERNATIONAL STUDIES, NORTHWESTERN UNIVERSITY

SPEND ONE OR TWO HOURS A DAY AT THE LIBRARY—that will make it possible for you to go out as much as you want and not cram too much.

SENIOR, INTERNATIONAL BUSINESS, XAVIER UNIVERSITY

It's really not all that hard to **balance work and play**. Just do your work before you play, and if you don't get it done, then you can't play! Your GPA might be your saving grace someday when applying to law school, med school, grad school. You might have an average/mediocre LSAT score, but an amazing GPA speaks loud and clear about what a hard worker and a talented student you really are.

SENIOR, GOVERNMENT, LAFAYETTE COLLEGE

You should expect to spend the same amount of time studying as you spend in class. And don't think that weekends are for hanging around; they are for STUDYING DURING THE DAY AND HAVING FUN AT NIGHT!

SENIOR, GOVERNMENT, UNIVERSITY OF VIRGINIA

ONCE UPON A CAMPUS

IT'S ALL IN THE PLANNING

JUST PLANNING OUT YOUR DAY or week can be a great help because it lets you know when you have meetings, when you have projects due, and also when you have time to hang out with your friends.

GRADUATE, ENVIRONMENTAL STUDIES, EMORY & HENRY COLLEGE

I always find it helpful to **have a calendar and write down when everything is due**. That way you're not waiting until the last minute to finish assignments, especially when you have multiple assignments due on one day or in one week.

GRADUATE, NEAR EASTERN AND JUDAIC STUDIES, BRANDEIS UNIVERSITY

MAKE A SCHEDULE AND STICK TO IT. It was not until my senior year when I had a full course load, GRE's, grad school applications, and a senior thesis to write, all in one semester, that I really learned how helpful this can be. It is an amazing life-saver. You get enough done and you keep moving rather than getting bogged down and overwhelmed.

GRADUATE, SOCIOLOGY, MILLS COLLEGE

I make a schedule and tell myself that I have to get through a certain amount of work before I go to bed each night. **It gets easier** as you get older, because everyone's majors get more demanding, so there are less people to fool around with.

SENIOR, BIOLOGY, BUCKNELL UNIVERSITY

TIME MANAGEMENT

"I don't need to study tonight—I'll do it in the morning when I get up at 5 a.m." YEAH, RIGHT!

GRADUATE, MASS COMMUNICATIONS, NORTHEASTERN STATE UNIVERSITY

My best papers were ones I wrote earlier than the day before they were due. If you do need to put off a paper until the night before it's due, at least do the readings for it or other prep work ahead of time.

SENIOR, ANTHROPOLOGY, UNIVERSITY OF TORONTO

I am in law school and there is **no room for procrastination.** If I had better work habits in college, law school would have been an easier transition.

GRADUATE, POLITICAL SCIENCE, ST. JOSEPH'S UNIVERSITY

I have been called the **"Queen of Procrastination."** I actually can't write papers ahead of time, unless the class requires me to turn in an outline and a rough draft. I tend to start essays at about 10 p.m. or 11 p.m. the night before they are due and pull an all-nighter. It sounds horrible, but I produce my best work when I'm under that kind of pressure.

GRADUATE, SOCIOLOGY, UNIVERSITY OF HAWAII—MANOA

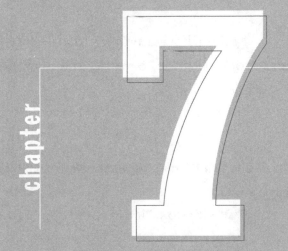

THE ART OF STUDYING

Throw on some sweatpants, turn off your cell phone, and get lost in the library.

SENIOR, POLITICAL SCIENCE/CHINESE LANGUAGE,
UNIVERSITY OF CALIFORNIA—IRVINE

THE ART OF STUDYING

I had a job where all I did was answer phones, and if I didn't have anything to do while I was there, I would go crazy! So, **I brought my homework with me to work,** and all I did was study in between phone calls. I got really good grades as a result.

SENIOR, PSYCHOLOGY, UNIVERSITY OF MARYLAND—COLLEGE PARK

The only class in which I aced both tests was one where MY STUDY GROUP met the night before each test in a bar. Whoever couldn't answer the questions had to buy a round.

GRADUATE, CORPORATE COMMUNICATIONS, UNIVERSITY OF HOUSTON

I'd go to a 24-hour diner far away from campus where I knew nobody else would be and stay till the sun came up.

GRADUATE, POLITICAL SCIENCE, UNIVERSITY OF CALIFORNIA—SAN DIEGO

If the thought of the sterile and prison-like library dissuaded me from my study plans, I would bring the books to **a cozy coffee shop** and make a point of enjoying it.

GRADUATE, INTERNATIONAL RELATIONS, BROWN UNIVERSITY

I'd go to a place in the library where I knew my friends would be so that we could all do work together. I made **SURE** we were all doing work and not just chatting!

GRADUATE, NEAR EASTERN AND JUDAIC STUDIES, BRANDEIS UNIVERSITY

I locked myself in the silent floors of the library. Once you get a couple of bad grades, it's not hard to force yourself to sit down and work.

SENIOR, GOVERNMENT, UNIVERSITY OF VIRGINIA

I sat among the stacks in the research library so there was nothing else to look at.

GRADUATE, JEWISH STUDIES, UNIVERSITY OF CALIFORNIA—LOS ANGELES

I went to the library or study lounge . . . when people around you are studying, it's easier to get motivated.

GRADUATE, ENGLISH/AMERICAN STUDIES, UNIVERSITY OF NOTRE DAME

Form study sessions even if you're the weak link. The top students always show up and everyone usually does well.

GRADUATE, ENGLISH, MOREHOUSE COLLEGE

Scheduling study groups is good because it forces you to look over the material before you meet, so you don't look stupid.

SENIOR, GOVERNMENT, UNIVERSITY OF VIRGINIA

Study groups were very beneficial to me since I tend to procrastinate when I'm by myself. **Meeting with a group of classmates** regularly keeps you on your toes because you never want to be the freeloader.

GRADUATE, MICROBIOLOGY/SOCIOLOGY, UNIVERSITY OF OKLAHOMA

I always had **study marathons** before midterms and finals. I would join study groups and we would all study for a few hours, then take a coffee break, then study for a few more hours. If you study with people you like, it is a lot more bearable, and sometimes it's even fun.

JUNIOR, BIOCHEMISTRY, UNIVERSITY OF CALIFORNIA—LOS ANGELES

I shut my computer off and went into SOLITARY CONFINEMENT.

GRADUATE, AMERICAN CIVILIZATIONS, BROWN UNIVERSITY

I cleared my mind and distanced myself from people who had other agendas. I surrounded myself with others who valued studying.

GRADUATE, ENGLISH, GEORGIA STATE UNIVERSITY

If you can manage to get up and **start your day at 7 a.m. or 8 a.m.** every day, it's like you have an eight-day week.

JUNIOR, HEALTH SCIENCE, NORTHEASTERN UNIVERSITY

I made sure that **I had incentives** like, "once I finish this I can take a break…" to get ice cream, watch a movie, or anything that sounded appealing.

SENIOR, PRE-LAW, UNIVERSITY OF ILLINOIS—URBANA-CHAMPAIGN

I MAKE A SCHEDULE WITH CHECK BOXES and check off each of the boxes as I finish my tasks. It always feels very rewarding to cross off something from my list!

SENIOR, LEGAL STUDIES/SOCIOLOGY, UNIVERSITY OF WISCONSIN

I would sit in my La-Z-Boy and I wouldn't let myself stop reading to go to the bathroom until I got through the chapter. You'd be amazed how fast you can read with a full bladder.

SENIOR, BIOLOGY, SEATTLE PACIFIC UNIVERSITY

The ideal situation is to be interested in the subject matter so that you are excited about studying. **If not, make school a game.** I would make bets with myself about what grade I could make on my next test.

GRADUATE, ENGLISH, TEXAS WOMEN'S UNIVERSITY

Study and then **take a long hot shower.** The shower gives you a chance to let the information mull around in your head, and the hot water seems to make the info soak into your brain.

SENIOR, BIOLOGY, MILLSAPS COLLEGE

My friends and I call it the "GROOVE TECHNIQUE": Just sit back for a second and groove with the music on your Discman or iPod as you reflect on the material you just read.

SENIOR, GENETICS, IOWA STATE UNIVERSITY

I forced myself to face THE PROSPECT OF FAILING and hated it so much that I just knew I had to sit and get through my studies.

SENIOR, PSYCHOLOGY, UNIVERSITY OF PENNSYLVANIA

Having the fear of making a bad grade forced me to study. Fear is a strong motivator.

JUNIOR, BIOLOGY, UNIVERSITY OF ILLINOIS—URBANA-CHAMPAIGN

Just thinking that my parents are shelling out gobs and gobs of money for me to be here is motivation enough. I don't want to have to deal with Dad—minus $25,000—when I get a D.

GRADUATE, CHEMICAL ENGINEERING, UNIVERSITY OF VIRGINIA

I remind myself that my GPA isn't so hot and I need to improve it to have **any chance of getting into grad school.** I also have a stuffed black cat with big yellow eyes sitting by my computer, staring at me, to scare me into studying when I'm tempted to goof off at the computer.

SENIOR, BIOCHEMISTRY/ENGLISH, UNIVERSITY OF CALIFORNIA—DAVIS

I KEEP MY GOALS VISUAL—whether it's my screen saver with a quote or a piece of paper with my name on it and the initials 'M.D.' written after it—anything to keep me on track toward reaching my goal.

JUNIOR, BIOLOGICAL SCIENCES, UNIVERSITY OF NEBRASKA—LINCOLN

REALITY BITES

I WORKED IN A FACTORY between my freshman and sophomore years. My dad reminded me that if I didn't finish college, that is where I would end up. That helped.

GRADUATE, BIOCHEMISTRY/SPANISH, UNIVERSITY OF WISCONSIN—MADISON

I chose the most pathetic adult in the family and then pictured myself being him.

JUNIOR, ACCOUNTING, CALIFORNIA STATE UNIVERSITY—SACRAMENTO

To force myself to study I would remind myself what **flipping burgers** at McDonald's would be like.

JUNIOR, BIOCHEMISTRY, VIRGINIA POLYTECHNIC INSTITUTE AND STATE UNIVERSITY

Wait for that particular inspiration called Last Minute Panic.

GRADUATE, BIOLOGY, UNIVERSITY OF VIRGINIA

TESTS AND PAPERS

A curve can work wonders, and if you don't seem any more clueless than anyone else in the class, you'll probably be okay.

SENIOR, ANTHROPOLOGY, UNIVERSITY OF TORONTO

"Over prepare" for your first round of tests.

GRADUATE, POLITICAL SCIENCE, TEXAS A&M UNIVERSITY

DON'T STRESS TOO MUCH. I had friends freshman year who nearly had nervous breakdowns, convincing themselves that every test would make or break the rest of their lives.

SENIOR, ANTHROPOLOGY, UNIVERSITY OF VERMONT

The first college exam you take is most likely going to kill you. It's normal. You use that painful realization and CHANNEL IT INTO MOTIVATION to prepare for the next one.

JUNIOR, BIOLOGY/CHEMISTRY, HOUSTON BAPTIST UNIVERSITY

Tutors are GREAT. Get them—and don't be embarrassed. In college the smart kids find tutors.

SENIOR, BIOCHEMISTRY AND MOLECULAR BIOLOGY, CORNELL COLLEGE

Start studying from day one and don't let up. Try to synthesize and apply the information, not memorize it.

JUNIOR, BIOLOGY, UNIVERSITY OF MICHIGAN—ANN ARBOR

TAKE A GOOD COMPOSITION CLASS at the beginning of school, because most of the tests are essay tests.

GRADUATE, LITERATURE, FLORIDA INTERNATIONAL UNIVERSITY

I think one of the most important things that I've learned is to **really listen and understand** during lectures. Don't just copy exactly what the professor says or writes, paraphrase to ensure your understanding. It really cuts down on time spent being confused later when you sit down and try to re-learn your notes.

JUNIOR, BIOLOGY AND CHEMISTRY, HOUSTON BAPTIST UNIVERSITY

Students should ask professors whether the focus of the test will be on the book, the notes, or both, and ask for study guides.

GRADUATE, SPEECH-LANGUAGE PATHOLOGY, TOWSON UNIVERSITY

Find the smart person in class and study with him. He will be easy to spot—he will ask questions and most likely take lots of notes. If you are the smart one, find someone who is having trouble—you will help someone and strengthen your own knowledge by explaining the concepts to your study partner.

GRADUATE, BIOPSYCHOLOGY, UNIVERSITY OF MICHIGAN

Talk to upperclassmen to get old examples of tests and papers.

GRADUATE, CLARINET PERFORMANCE, VASSAR COLLEGE

Figure out how to write a college paper as soon as possible. This includes actually coming up with something interesting/original to say, picking out quotes from the text, and for extra pizzazz, adding quotes from outside sources and using beautiful vocabulary and sentence structure.

GRADUATE, ETHNIC STUDIES/HISTORY, BROWN UNIVERSITY

UTILIZE THE WRITING CENTER on your campus. Those people have experience in writing and can definitely help you improve your writing skills and papers.

GRADUATE, NEAR EASTERN AND JUDAIC STUDIES, BRANDEIS UNIVERSITY

Ask for help from teachers. Ask them for examples of what they're looking for ("So what would an 'A' paper look like?").

GRADUATE, PSYCHOLOGY, UNIVERSITY OF ALABAMA

Don't write exactly what the teacher said. ADD YOUR OWN THOUGHTS to the mix.

GRADUATE, HISTORY/ANTHROPOLOGY, UNIVERSITY OF PENNSYLVANIA

Take advantage of **writing centers** that are there, and free, to help students write papers.

GRADUATE, BIOLOGY, CLEMSON UNIVERSITY

LEARN HOW TO WRITE during your first semester in college. Invest time in your freshman writing course! Writing in college is completely different from high school, and the most common comments from freshmen are about how their high school teachers loved their writing, but now in college they are doing horribly on their writing assignments.

GRADUATE, SPEECH-LANGUAGE PATHOLOGY, TOWSON UNIVERSITY

DON'T BE AFRAID TO ASK professors about rough drafts, but be an active asker. Don't just hand in a rough draft. Ask questions about your style, choice of words, etc.

GRADUATE, GOVERNMENT/GERMAN STUDIES, SMITH COLLEGE

Always have at least two other people (preferably older and with more writing experience than you) help you revise your papers before turning them in.

GRADUATE, BIOCHEMISTRY/SPANISH, UNIVERSITY OF WISCONSIN—MADISON

Go to professors with a rough draft and ASK FOR COMMENTS before handing in the final product.

GRADUATE, AMERICAN CIVILIZATIONS, BROWN UNIVERSITY

Set your own deadline for three to five days before the paper is actually due. On that day have a FINAL draft completed. Leave it alone for a day or two and then come back to it. This will give you perspective on your own work and help you avoid writing the paper all on the last night.

GRADUATE, BIOPSYCHOLOGY, UNIVERSITY OF MICHIGAN

In college, there are only two or three tests and/or papers in a semester-long class, so you have to do really well on all of them to do well in the class. YOU HAVE TO BE PREPARED enough to know how the professor is going to ask you questions on a test or how the professor wants you to write a paper from the very start.

JUNIOR, COGNITIVE SCIENCE, UNIVERSITY OF VIRGINIA

Never turn in a paper that hasn't been proofread by two or three people. You may think you're error-free, but you'll be surprised by what you overlooked the night before while dozing off at the computer.

GRADUATE, ENGLISH, MOREHOUSE COLLEGE

My number one rule for myself is to **go to class**. No matter what. If I go to class consistently and take good notes, tests will be doable. No matter how little I read the texts—or even studied—if I went to class, I at least got a passing grade.

SENIOR, HISTORY, LOYOLA MARYMOUNT UNIVERSITY

Go to class. **Going to the lectures** will let you know exactly what information is important. If you don't go to class, you are on your own. I also recommend re-copying lecture notes. I was given this tip at college orientation and it worked for me.

GRADUATE, GOVERNMENT AND POLITICS, UNIVERSITY OF MARYLAND—COLLEGE PARK

9

PROFESSORS

Don't ask stupid questions . . . and there are stupid questions.

SENIOR, HISTORY, UNIVERSITY OF NOTRE DAME

JUST YOUR AVERAGE JOE

COLLEGE PROFESSORS ARE NORMAL PEOPLE. Some are kind, some are jerks, some are smart, some are brilliant, some are awful teachers, some are superb instructors. And you have to accept that and approach them accordingly. TAs are mutants; cross your fingers and hope they're normal.

JUNIOR, PHILOSOPHY, NORTHWESTERN UNIVERSITY

Professors and teacher's assistants genuinely care that you're learning. They're not there to ruin your life (a misconception we all had in high school). They're there because they are passionate about what they're teaching you, and they want you to see why they love what they're teaching. Show them that **you care about what you're learning**, not just to get a good grade but because you're interested in the subject.

GRADUATE, BIOMETRY AND STATISTICS, CORNELL UNIVERSITY

Most professors truly want to help you; however there are those who seem like they want nothing more than to watch you fail. Don't let those professors get you down. **Work harder to succeed** despite them. Trust me, it feels good when you do.

SENIOR, BIOLOGY, MARY WASHINGTON COLLEGE

Just because they're great lecturers doesn't mean they have **great people skills**. And just because they're bad lecturers doesn't mean they have **bad people skills.**

GRADUATE, POLITICAL SCIENCE, UNIVERSITY OF CALIFORNIA—SAN DIEGO

PROFESSORS LIKE TO HAVE FEEDBACK when teaching a class. They also like to know that the students are prepared for the class.

SENIOR, BIOCHEMISTRY, LEHMAN COLLEGE

Professors want respect. If your professor has a Ph.D., you should remember that when you address him.

GRADUATE, BUSINESS ADMINISTRATION, UNIVERSITY OF FLORIDA

Show you're trying, even if it's an email before a test asking a question you already know the answer to. They love **feeling like they are important** and actually teaching you things outside of the classroom.

GRADUATE, SOCIOLOGY/FAMILY STUDIES AND HUMAN DEVELOPMENT, UNIVERSITY OF ARIZONA

Respect their time; they really have a lot of other things to do. DON'T GO TO OFFICE HOURS UNPREPARED.

SENIOR, CHEMISTRY, CORNELL UNIVERSITY

Do not approach a professor by asking what will be on the test. It is saying that you are only interested in the grade and not **the process of learning**.

GRADUATE, BIOCHEMISTRY, UNIVERSITY OF CALIFORNIA—DAVIS

Be early to class— walking in late is very rude. I was amazed by how many times I saw students walk in late right in front of a professor while she was lecturing. The professor didn't like this at all. It is also rude to leave class before the lecture is over.

GRADUATE, ECONOMICS/GOVERNMENT AND POLITICS, UNIVERSITY OF MARYLAND—COLLEGE PARK

ASSISTED LEARNING

While the professors may be busy doing research and working for tenure, the **TAs are an untapped source of information** and are almost always willing to give you advice, whether it be on courses, professors, or just campus life in general.

GRADUATE, PSYCHOLOGY AND SOCIAL BEHAVIOR, UNIVERSITY OF CALIFORNIA—IRVINE

TAs ARE USUALLY COOL and will help you out a lot. Professors' office hours are helpful, but don't go if you are clueless about a subject—stick with the TA. You don't want to look bad in front of the person who is going to give you the grade.

JUNIOR, BIOCHEMISTRY, UNIVERSITY OF CALIFORNIA—LOS ANGELES

TAs are just like you and, for the most part, they truly have **a passion for what they're teaching.** Relate to them on an equal level.

GRADUATE, LEGAL STUDIES, UNIVERSITY OF MASSACHUSETTS—AMHERST

Make your professors and TAs **talk to you at your level** and be honest if you don't understand something.

GRADUATE, BIOLOGY, SEATTLE UNIVERSITY

If you're drowning, talk to your professor EARLY IN THE SEMESTER. It will make the difference.

GRADUATE, HISTORY, RUTGERS UNIVERSITY

ONCE UPON A CAMPUS

95

If you ask for help, you'll usually get it—probably more than you asked for.

GRADUATE, POLITICAL SCIENCE, UNIVERSITY OF THE SOUTH

You need to know who grades your work, and go to that person for help. For example, if the professor lectures, but the TA is the one who does all the grading, go to the TA for help with any assignments.

GRADUATE, SOCIOLOGY, UNIVERSITY OF HAWAII—MANOA

Professors and TAs are pretty accommodating, so make sure that you have good communication with them. They are not mind-readers so you have to take the initiative and explain your problem, and most of the time you will be pleased with the result!

GRADUATE, BIOCHEMISTRY, RUTGERS UNIVERSITY

They sometimes forget what it was like to be in our position, so TALK TO THEM FREQUENTLY and they will more often take into account your problems and concerns.

SENIOR, BIOCHEMISTRY/PSYCHOLOGY, BAYLOR UNIVERSITY

You have to communicate. Otherwise, they just won't know the difficulties you are facing. Meet with them, email them, leave them notes—whatever it takes.

SENIOR, PSYCHOLOGY, UNIVERSITY OF PENNSYLVANIA

PROFESSORS

A professor will not flunk you if he knows your name.

GRADUATE, SPORTS MANAGEMENT, UNIVERSITY OF KANSAS

Be opinionated! Don't just say yes to everything professors and TAs say; they could be wrong sometimes, and if you correct their mistakes, they will actually remember you!

JUNIOR, BIOLOGY, BINGHAMTON UNIVERSITY

You really just need to GET PROFESSORS AND TEACHER'S ASSISTANTS TO NOTICE YOU. Let them know that regardless of your status in class, you are willing to go the extra mile to do better and you are open to their ideas.

GRADUATE, POLITICAL SCIENCE, UNIVERSITY OF HAWAII—MANOA

Email is the greatest invention ever. It's just so much easier to get your questions answered right away.

JUNIOR, BIOLOGY, COLLEGE OF WILLIAM & MARY

If you show enthusiasm in your instructor's fields or in what they are teaching you, then it will be easy to get their attention. Sit up in front and right in the middle of the lecture hall. If you are really interested in the subject or lecture, use physical communication to show it. Smile and nod your head to show you understand what is being said. Although a freshman might not think it's important for the lecturer to know that she exists, **establishing a relationship with one's instructors is very important**, and it will pay off tremendously once the time comes to ask those instructors for letters of recommendation to get into grad school.

SENIOR, PSYCHOLOGY/SOCIAL BEHAVIOR, UNIVERSITY OF CALIFORNIA—IRVINE

HONESTY IS THE BEST POLICY

If you aren't going to be in class, make it a point to write a quick email to your professor. And when you get back to class, make it a point to talk to the professor about what you have missed and explain that you are concerned about falling behind. They will get to know your name, and they will see that you are truly concerned about the course.

GRADUATE, ENGLISH, GEORGE MASON UNIVERSITY

Be honest. If you missed a class because you slept through it, tell them! They won't be entirely happy, but they'll know that you aren't a liar.

GRADUATE, ENVIRONMENTAL STUDIES, EMORY & HENRY COLLEGE

Never miss an opportunity to ask other students which professors they have taken classes from and what they thought about the professors and the classes. A good professor is the most important factor in choosing classes, and information from former students is the most valuable resource when choosing classes.

SENIOR, POLITICAL SCIENCE, UNIVERSITY OF CALIFORNIA—SAN DIEGO

The seniors and juniors can advise you on who the best professors are. Don't just sign up for classes with the lenient professors, take classes where **the professors will actually teach you something.** You're an adult now, try to think about the long term. You might just have to use this information sometime in another class.

GRADUATE, BIOLOGY, UNIVERSITY OF CENTRAL FLORIDA

You should try to get in contact with any recent alumni or current students of the school that you will be attending to pick their brains and GET THE BACKGROUND ON CERTAIN PROFESSORS.

GRADUATE, ENGLISH/MUSIC, THE COLLEGE OF WILLIAM & MARY

Check out a publication like CAPE (Course and Professor Evaluations), a book put out by a student-run organization that gives approval ratings of every course and professor, including how many hours of work per week, difficulty of exams, and other things students had to say about their classes.

GRADUATE, PSYCHOLOGY, UNIVERSITY OF CALIFORNIA—SAN DIEGO

You should read the course descriptions, know something about the professor, and KNOW WHAT YOU'RE GETTING INTO for each class. It saves hassles later on during the semester.

GRADUATE, SOCIOLOGY, UNIVERSITY OF HAWAII—MANOA

GAIN THE EXTRA ADVANTAGE

The more your professor knows you, the better. My relationship came in handy when I had an emergency and could not turn something in right on time or could not make it to class.

GRADUATE, POLITICAL SCIENCE/ENGLISH, SPELMAN COLLEGE

I am thankful that I formed relationships with my professors. When all is said and done and you've received your degree, they still have an impact on your future. Applying to law or grad schools with a letter of recommendation from Professor Joe Shmoe, who "thinks he remembers you," is useless.

GRADUATE, SOCIAL RELATIONS, JAMES MADISON COLLEGE AT MICHIGAN STATE UNIVERSITY

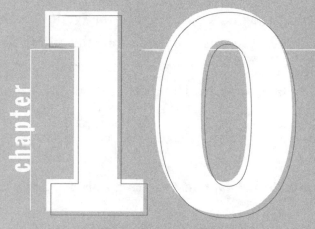

COURSES AND MAJORS

You have to ask yourself, "What class is going to get me out of bed at eight o'clock in the morning?" That is a class you should definitely sign up for

SENIOR, BIOMEDICAL SCIENCES,
MARQUETTE UNIVERSITY

I firmly believe that you go to college to grow academically, socially, and individually. Therefore I think it is imperative to take classes that further your personal interests as much as your academic interests, even if it means you don't graduate within four years. College is supposed to be "the time of your life" and you should have no regrets, so indulging your curiosities is as important as fulfilling your academic curriculum—take a history of film class if it pleases your heart.

SENIOR, JOURNALISM, UNIVERSITY OF TEXAS—AUSTIN

This is college; FIND WHAT YOU LOVE AND DO IT. If you're not sure what you love, maintain variety and you'll find it.

GRADUATE, POLITICAL SCIENCE, COLORADO STATE UNIVERSITY

Pick courses that will still be interesting two-and-a-half months into the semester. If it doesn't sound interesting in August, just think how much you'll hate it in November.

SENIOR, PHILOSOPHY, STATE UNIVERSITY OF NEW YORK—ALBANY

Screw practicality. **Take classes you'll enjoy.** No major is going to prepare you for a job.

GRADUATE, FILM, BRIGHAM YOUNG UNIVERSITY

Ask yourself: "Is this going to be beneficial to my future career?" "Is this going to be beneficial to my understanding of the world?" **"What interests me most?"** "Will I be challenged?"

GRADUATE, BIOLOGY, SAINT JOSEPH'S UNIVERSITY

Pick classes where you are going to use the information. Don't pick silly things like French Basket Weaving—what is that going to do for you later?

GRADUATE, HEALTH AND SOCIETY, UNIVERSITY OF ROCHESTER

When picking courses, especially hard ones, I stop and think: down the road, will I regret not taking this class just because it is hard and I don't want to work that much? Don't let laziness now make you regretful later.

SENIOR, BIOLOGY, COLLEGE OF WILLIAM & MARY

HAVE A DESIRE TO LEARN THE SUBJECT MATTER—if you don't like the topic, it doesn't matter how good the teacher is; you won't get anything out of doing the work.

SENIOR, FILM, NORTHWESTERN UNIVERSITY

You are going to have to take an 8 a.m. class, so accept it. An 8 a.m. class with a "good" professor is better than a noon class with a "bad" one.

GRADUATE, BIOLOGY, COLLEGE OF CHARLESTON

MAJOR REQUIREMENTS

Find out **EXACTLY what your major requires**, then meet with an advisor and work out your entire schedule for the next four years. That way you don't end up with tons of useless classes and have to spend five years catching up.

SENIOR, POLITICAL SCIENCE, UNIVERSITY OF CALIFORNIA—DAVIS

Planning out my major helped a lot when the enrollment period came around. Try to anticipate little surprises. For example, smaller schools don't offer every course every year, so plan ahead. No one wants to get to senior year and find out that a required class won't be offered that year.

SENIOR, BIOLOGY/PRE-MEDICINE AND VOCATIONAL MINISTRY, OKLAHOMA CHRISTIAN UNIVERSITY

Once you figure out your major, TAKE THE REQUISITE COURSES. I could have graduated early, but I was not able to enroll in all of the classes I needed because in my freshman year I took more of a broad curriculum instead of being more focused on my major.

GRADUATE, INTERNATIONAL STUDIES/RUSSIAN, JOHNS HOPKINS UNIVERSITY

Always make sure EVERY class you take fulfills a major requirement. And never think that because a class is on the mating habits of tsetse flies that it can't be really fun; they often are.

GRADUATE, ANTHROPOLOGY, ARIZONA STATE UNIVERSITY

It is very important to make sure that if **you're taking a class to fulfill a requirement**, it actually fills the requirement. My friends and I have completed horrible classes only to realize that we didn't even need to take them.

SENIOR, COMMUNICATIONS, ARIZONA STATE UNIVERSITY

I came into college as a business major because I thought it was a good route to take. WRONG! I ended up taking classes I wasn't interested in and therefore, I did horribly, which killed my GPA. So if you're not sure what you want to do, there's **nothing wrong with saying that your major is "undecided."**

SENIOR, FAMILY STUDIES, MIAMI UNIVERSITY

My biggest regret was not having a set direction in college. For the first two years, I had no clue what I wanted to do. By the time I made up my mind, I had to take all the courses for my major at the same time. So my last two years were all the difficult courses.

GRADUATE, ECONOMICS, NEW YORK UNIVERSITY

I will soon be entering medical school and I thought that as a pre-med major you had to major in science. However, that is not the case. I will be taking science for the rest of my life so I SHOULD HAVE DONE SOMETHING DIFFERENT at the time.

GRADUATE, BIOLOGY, HOUGHTON COLLEGE

ALL IN THE TIMING

Are you really going to be able to make **an 8 a.m. class?**

GRADUATE, LEGAL STUDIES, UNIVERSITY OF MASSACHUSETTS —AMHERST

Always get morning classes if possible. That way, you will have the rest of the day to study or hang out, and it feels like more time is available than when you're cramming for afternoon classes.

GRADUATE, ENGLISH, MOREHOUSE COLLEGE

UNLIKE MOST STUDENTS, I LIKE TO SPREAD MY CLASSES OUT THROUGHOUT THE DAY. I find this gives me time to study or complete work in between classes, and let's face it, I also have nothing better to do.

GRADUATE, BUSINESS ADMINISTRATION, UNIVERSITY OF FLORIDA

Think about how much time you have between classes and other commitments rather than trying to always end up with four-day weekends. You can use this time to study, instead of wasting four days trying to force yourself to study. This way you have **a ready-made study schedule.**

GRADUATE, ECONOMICS, STATE UNIVERSITY OF NEW YORK—STONY BROOK

Avoid big gaps in your schedule. It's nice to be able to go onto campus once and come back after your classes are all done.

GRADUATE, MOLECULAR CELL BIOLOGY, UNIVERSITY OF CALIFORNIA—BERKELEY

Try to **spread out the classes you'll really like** with the ones you know you'll hate, so you won't have extreme burnout semesters with nothing but difficult, boring classes.

GRADUATE, PSYCHOLOGY, EAST TENNESSEE STATE UNIVERSITY

Spend your first quarter adjusting; take a moderate amount of units your first year; take your second and third years very seriously (load up on units); THEN RELAX YOUR LAST YEAR.

SENIOR, POLITICAL SCIENCE/CHINESE LANGUAGE, UNIVERSITY OF CALIFORNIA—IRVINE

I made the mistake of taking all of my general requirements in the first two years and when I became an upperclassman, I was stuck with all my high-level classes at once. It is difficult to raise your GPA when you have all biology classes in one quarter. **I should have consulted my advisor more,** but I thought I knew what I was doing on my own.

JUNIOR, BIOLOGY, OHIO STATE UNIVERSITY

Balance hard classes with easier ones or creative ones with technical ones or science classes with literature classes. It's so important to take a variety of classes, because when the exams kick in, it's more refreshing to switch from a paper in one subject to one in another.

GRADUATE, INTERNATIONAL RELATIONS, BROWN UNIVERSITY

DON'T TAKE THE MOST TIME-CONSUMING CLASSES ALL IN ONE SEMESTER. I, for example, learned the hard way when I signed up for three writing component classes at once and ended up having to withdraw from one mid-semester.

GRADUATE, PSYCHOLOGY, UNIVERSITY OF TEXAS—AUSTIN

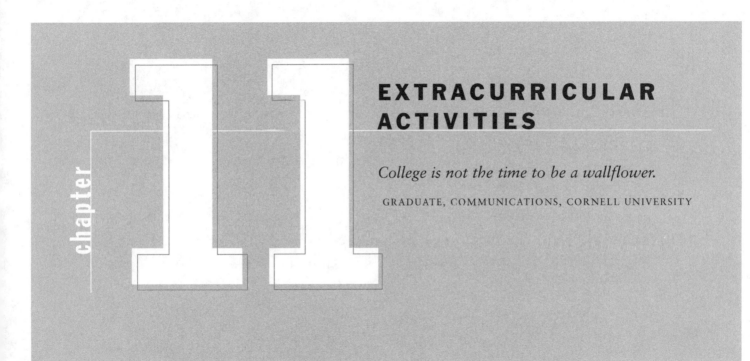

11

EXTRACURRICULAR ACTIVITIES

College is not the time to be a wallflower.

GRADUATE, COMMUNICATIONS, CORNELL UNIVERSITY

BIRDS OF A FEATHER

Check the bulletin boards for a club or an event where you can meet others with similar interests.

GRADUATE, ENGLISH/FRENCH, CORNELL UNIVERSITY

Being a student is only part of my life—I have to involve myself in other activities to **keep myself balanced** and to maintain my perspective.

SENIOR, BUSINESS ADMINISTRATION, ROANOKE COLLEGE

I suggest going to as many different meetings as possible. Even if you're only remotely interested in the club, it might present something that will convince you it's worth your time.

GRADUATE, SOCIOLOGY, UNIVERSITY OF CALIFORNIA—IRVINE

You will never again have **the opportunity to do so many varied things** or have access to the kinds of resources that a university offers. Take advantage.

SENIOR, PRE-MEDICINE AND VOCATIONAL MINISTRY, OKLAHOMA CHRISTIAN UNIVERSITY

Some people say major partying is the way to collegiate social success, but **the more enduring bonds you will form** are via clubs and organizations.

SENIOR, GENDER STUDIES/RELIGIOUS STUDIES, BROWN UNIVERSITY

BE ALL YOU CAN BE

I organized free backpacking, ice climbing, horsepacking, kayaking, skiing and snowboarding trips, and art tours for fellow students through a grant given to the college. I loved to make people **focus on things other than school** by throwing wonderful trips at them.

GRADUATE, BIOCHEMISTRY/MOLECULAR BIOLOGY, REED COLLEGE

I participated in the ballroom dance club and kickboxing, and I tutored. **I wanted to keep a balance** between my academic interests and my physical fitness.

GRADUATE, PSYCHOLOGY, UNIVERSITY OF TEXAS—AUSTIN

EXTRACURRICULAR ACTIVITIES are like a buffet: try a little bit of this and a little bit of that. Don't join anything right away—give each option some time so that you can decide what interests you enough to pursue further.

SENIOR, POLITICAL SCIENCE, UNIVERSITY OF NOTRE DAME

I PARTICIPATED IN STUDENT GOVERNMENT. I really like to argue and I also wanted to get involved, so Student Senate sounded great. After two years as a senator, I eventually became my university's student body president. It will be a while before I get to be the CEO of a half-a-million dollar a year organization again.

SENIOR, BIOLOGY/CHEMISTRY, SEATTLE PACIFIC UNIVERSITY

I founded the Free Burma Coalition at my school. By working on this cause independently, I felt I was doing something more worthwhile. I also worked at the radio station—I thought it was an excellent and educational way to have fun. Plus, I was exposed to more of the 'real world' when doing promotions away from campus.

GRADUATE, INTERNATIONAL RELATIONS, BROWN UNIVERSITY

ACADEMIC ASPIRATIONS

It's good to pursue leadership roles and **participate in community service** because it'll look excellent on your resume or applications for professional schools—and it's fun and a great way to meet new people who share the same interests as you.

SENIOR, PSYCHOLOGY, UNIVERSITY OF ALABAMA—HUNTSVILLE

I am involved in a lot of organizations related to engineering. I participate in these organizations because most of my time is spent with my classmates and with doing work related to our major. Being in organizations that are related to my major gives me a voice in what happens within the school and my department.

JUNIOR, BIOMEDICAL ENGINEERING AND PRE-MEDICINE, SAINT LOUIS UNIVERSITY

I'm a political science major and I plan on going to law school. I JOINED ACADEMIC CLUBS like the Pre-Law Society early and knew more about applying to law school as a second-year than graduating seniors.

SENIOR, POLITICAL SCIENCE/CHINESE LANGUAGE, UNIVERSITY OF CALIFORNIA—IRVINE

Extracurriculars get you away from the television and add structure and balance to your life.

GRADUATE, BUSINESS ADMINISTRATION, MOREHOUSE COLLEGE

Playing intramural sports is great because you do just as much socializing as you do practicing—it's much more low key than a varsity sport but you still have a great time and get exercise.

SENIOR, MATHEMATICAL ECONOMICS, COLGATE UNIVERSITY

I always loved sports but I didn't have the time (or talent) to play for a Division I team. Instead, I joined a bunch of intramural leagues that were a blast and also A GREAT WAY TO MEET PEOPLE WHO SHARED MY INTERESTS.

SENIOR, LEGAL STUDIES, QUINNIPIAC UNIVERSITY

My most memorable experience was **being on the baseball field every day**, knowing I was working harder and doing more than the typical college student.

GRADUATE, POLITICAL SCIENCE, UNIVERSITY OF THE SOUTH

A REAL WORLD OF PROBLEMS

I have been a mentor for inner-city African American males and a member of Noon Run, an organization that makes and serves lunches to the homeless. I wanted to take advantage of the diverse culture that Milwaukee offers and interact with people that I normally would never meet.

SENIOR, BIOMEDICAL SCIENCES, MARQUETTE UNIVERSITY

I work in a crisis center because I am extremely interested in psychology and want to practice my empathy skills.

SENIOR, PSYCHOLOGY, UNIVERSITY OF MICHIGAN

I participated in many identity groups such as the Women of Color Collective and Ujamaa, a group for African American students. I think it's important for minority students to form support groups, especially during college. There are still a lot of issues that the disabled students, homosexual students, and students of color have to face that are not understood by the majority.

GRADUATE, NEUROSCIENCE AND BEHAVIOR, WESLEYAN UNIVERSITY

I worked as a peer counselor for victims of sexual assault, which was a problem on our campus.

GRADUATE, GOVERNMENT, DARTMOUTH COLLEGE

I volunteered at the health clinic to see if I really wanted to be pre-med.

SENIOR, CHEMISTRY, CORNELL UNIVERSITY

I volunteered at the hospital in a pediatric unit, participated in a biology club and the pre-med club, and worked in two research labs. I did these things to help me get into medical school.

SENIOR, PRE-MEDICINE/PSYCHOLOGY, UNIVERSITY OF IOWA

ONCE UPON A CAMPUS

I played soccer with Special Olympic athletes for two fall semesters as a community service project connected to my school. I did that since I knew it would be fun, and it was something I'd never tried before. Playing soccer for S.O. was probably the most fun experience I've had in college.

SENIOR, HEALTH ADMINISTRATION AND POLICY, UNIVERSITY OF MARYLAND

I AM INVOLVED IN A NATIONAL SERVICE FRATERNITY, which is not only personally fulfilling, but also benefits others.

JUNIOR, BIOMEDICAL ENGINEERING/PRE-MEDICINE, SAINT LOUIS UNIVERSITY

I pledged a sorority, and it was the best thing I did throughout my college career. It opened so many doors and introduced me to my very best friends. I would recommend it to anyone.

GRADUATE, MASS COMMUNICATIONS, NORTHEASTERN STATE UNIVERSITY

In actuality I never imagined joining a fraternity, but once I met the other guys there, we all clicked and **it made sense to join** since I hung out with them a great deal anyway.

GRADUATE, INTERNATIONAL STUDIES/RUSSIAN, JOHNS HOPKINS UNIVERSITY

My most memorable experiences involved just **hanging out in my fraternity house** with all my friends. Spring break in Amsterdam with nine of my fraternity brothers was one of the greatest times of my life.

GRADUATE, ECONOMICS/PHILOSOPHY, STATE UNIVERSITY OF NEW YORK—BINGHAMTON

I was in a business fraternity. I joined at first for networking, but I have also made so many new friends and participated in so many activities.

GRADUATE, BUSINESS ADMINISTRATION, UNIVERSITY OF MISSOURI—COLUMBIA

I was in a sorority because it was **a good way to get involved**, both socially and within the community. Also, networking with alumni to find a job was important!

SENIOR, ANTHROPOLOGY/INTERNATIONAL STUDIES, NORTHWESTERN UNIVERSITY

I am in a sorority because I LOVE THAT I FEEL LIKE I'M AT CAMP when I'm really at school!

SENIOR, PSYCHOLOGY, UNIVERSITY OF MICHIGAN

Fraternities and sororities are also good sources for getting old exams to study from for your classes.

GRADUATE, HISTORY, COLGATE UNIVERSITY

For some people **IT'S BETTER TO WAIT UNTIL SOPHOMORE YEAR** than to rush a fraternity or sorority as a freshman. How can you possibly say, "I want to be a member of this organization for four years" based on one week of interaction with the members?

SENIOR, ECONOMICS, DEPAUW UNIVERSITY

chapter

12

NEW FRIENDS

When all else fails, start baking cookies.
New friends will flock to you.

SENIOR, MARKETING, UNIVERSITY OF NOTRE DAME

Find an activity you're interested in and go participate in it. It doesn't matter if it's academic, athletic, or something else. If the activity interests you, you'll likely find people who interest you there.

GRADUATE, INFORMATICS, UNIVERSITY OF WASHINGTON

Attend events that support issues that you are adamant about—it's the best way to find people who share the same interests as you.

GRADUATE, POLITICAL ECONOMY OF INDUSTRIAL SOCIETIES, UNIVERSITY OF CALIFORNIA—BERKELEY

The best way to meet people in college is to get involved!

Only in college will you find so many young people in one place who all want to meet people with similar interests.

GRADUATE, BIOLOGY/NUTRITION, PENNSYLVANIA STATE UNIVERSITY

NEW FRIENDS

The first few weeks of school is **the time to go to the parties** that you normally wouldn't go to . . . that's when everyone goes. Meet people that way; then you can settle into your own little niche.

GRADUATE, CHEMICAL ENGINEERING, UNIVERSITY OF VIRGINIA

MEET THE PEOPLE AROUND YOU in your first year. After that it keeps getting harder because everyone is already associated with another group of friends.

GRADUATE, BIOLOGY/ENGLISH, INDIANA UNIVERSITY—BLOOMINGTON

I JUST SAID 'HI' AND TRIED TO TALK TO AS MANY PEOPLE AS I COULD—even if it was just small talk—for the first couple of days, especially people in my dorm or classes. Eventually, you discover who you really enjoy talking to.

GRADUATE, SOCIOLOGY, UNIVERSITY OF HAWAII—MANOA

I met people by talking to anyone and everyone that I found remotely interesting in any one of my classes. It may be difficult to do at first, and some of the people you approach may not take to it well, but in the long run it definitely pays off.

GRADUATE, PSYCHOLOGY, XAVIER UNIVERSITY

Network. Use people you meet in class and your dorm to meet people they know—try not to pass up the opportunity to go out with a new group of people.

SENIOR, ANTHROPOLOGY, UNIVERSITY OF TORONTO

INTELLECTUAL EQUALS

Sit next to people you think are interesting and STRIKE UP A CONVERSATION about the class.

SENIOR, PSYCHOLOGY, FLORIDA ATLANTIC UNIVERSITY

Be outgoing: be the first one to talk in class when the TA asks you to break into groups. It's easy to stay outgoing when you start, but when you start out quiet, it's tough to switch roles.

GRADUATE, POLITICAL SCIENCE/SOCIOLOGY/LEGAL STUDIES, UNIVERSITY OF WISCONSIN—MADISON

The best way to meet people in college is through study groups and social activities. Always be the person in class that anyone could ask for help in that particular subject, and you will automatically become popular.

GRADUATE, ENGLISH, MOREHOUSE COLLEGE

Talk! People are like animals—If you leave them alone, they'll leave you alone.

GRADUATE, PHYSICS, GROSSMONT COLLEGE

FIND PEOPLE SITTING ALONE in dining halls and after introducing yourself, sit down to eat with them.

GRADUATE, ENGLISH, CORNELL UNIVERSITY

Be outgoing and smile—don't be afraid to put yourself out there.

SENIOR, PSYCHOLOGY, UNIVERSITY OF MICHIGAN

He bought a Playstation 2 and let me play it all the time.

JUNIOR, ACCOUNTING, WASHINGTON UNIVERSITY

We lay down on our dorm room floor and sang every song that came to mind at the top of our lungs for 30 minutes straight.

SENIOR, PSYCHOLOGY/ CRIMINOLOGY, FLORIDA STATE UNIVERSITY

He had the guts to say he could not understand a word the professor was saying.

GRADUATE, POLITICS, NEW YORK UNIVERSITY

She wouldn't leave my room.

GRADUATE, BIOLOGY, UNIVERSITY OF CALIFORNIA—LOS ANGELES

I bailed him out of jail.

SENIOR, ENGLISH, ROLLINS COLLEGE

I started looking at my other friendships more critically. Once you have a really true friend, your standards for friendship rise.

GRADUATE, INTERNATIONAL RELATIONS, BROWN UNIVERSITY

Most people are not quick to do you any favors, but the ones who do are **your true friends**.

GRADUATE, ENGLISH, UNIVERSITY OF FLORIDA

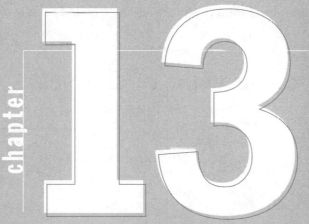

chapter

13

SIGNIFICANT (OR NOT-SO-SIGNIFICANT) OTHERS: Dating in College

Word travels fast around campus, so don't do anything you don't want to hear about from your neighbor's lab partner's best friend the next day!

GRADUATE, PSYCHOLOGY, MUHLENBERG COLLEGE

Beware of **"beer goggles."** They make a person look ten times more attractive than they really are.

GRADUATE, ACCOUNTING, VIRGINIA POLYTECHNIC INSTITUTE AND STATE UNIVERSITY

Drunken hookups are a part of college, so relish the walk of shame!

GRADUATE, ECONOMICS, CORNELL UNIVERSITY

If you're really drunk, don't let someone talk you into going home with them. Find a friend and stick with them instead.

SENIOR, ENVIRONMENTAL STUDIES, MIDDLEBURY COLLEGE

SIGNIFICANT (OR NOT-SO-SIGNIFICANT) OTHERS

GENERAL GUIDELINES

Generally, it helps to KNOW THE PERSON'S NAME before you hook up with them. Chances are, you're going to run into them again.

JUNIOR, BIOLOGICAL SCIENCES, RUTGERS UNIVERSITY

Don't kiss and tell. If you do, people won't just start talking about the person you kissed— they'll start talking about you, too.

GRADUATE, CHEMICAL ENGINEERING, UNIVERSITY OF RHODE ISLAND

STAY PROTECTED! The old "it won't happen to me" attitude is totally immature and unsafe.

SENIOR, HISTORY, FORDHAM UNIVERSITY

If you're going to have a guest spend the night in your room, make sure to **inform your roommate**. Many an awkward situation has occurred when people don't follow this rule.

GRADUATE, COMMUNICATIONS, CORNELL UNIVERSITY

It isn't the best idea to hook up with someone in one of your classes. Because if it doesn't work out, it can get awkward when you have to sit next to them for 55 minutes three times a week.

GRADUATE, CHEMISTRY, UNIVERSITY OF CHICAGO

Don't confuse hooking up with dating. It's easy to get your feelings hurt in college when one person thinks they're in a relationship and the other just thinks he or she is having a good time.

GRADUATE, ENGLISH, PRINCETON UNIVERSITY

If you unexpectedly go home with a guy or a girl, MAKE SURE TO TELL YOUR FRIENDS so that they're not looking for you all night and they know where you'll be the next day.

SENIOR, LITERATURE, BARNARD COLLEGE

Forget about any long distance relationship you started in high school. It sounds harsh, but chances are, it's not going to last.

SENIOR, WRITING, EMERSON COLLEGE

LONG DISTANCE RELATIONSHIPS ARE DIFFICULT, but you can make them last if the feelings are mutual.

SOPHOMORE, MECHANICAL ENGINEERING, UNIVERSITY OF EVANSVILLE

KEEP YOUR EYE ON THE BALL

Having a boyfriend/girlfriend is great, but **don't get involved with a slacker** who will keep you from studying.

JUNIOR, PHARMACOLOGY, UNIVERSITY OF CONNECTICUT

It's exciting to have a boyfriend or girlfriend at college because you can spend all your time with that person. But don't! There are new friends to make, clubs to join, and opportunities to explore. Don't get so wrapped up in your relationship that you miss it all.

GRADUATE, ART, UNIVERSITY OF HAWAII—MANOA

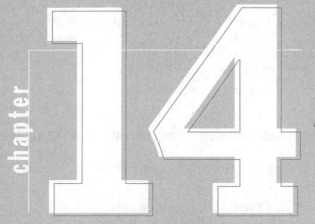

DINING DOS AND DON'TS

Practice eating cardboard to prepare for the food in the dining hall.

SENIOR, BIOLOGY, STATE UNIVERSITY OF
NEW YORK, BUFFALO

TRICKS OF THE TRADE

Never buy a meal plan that doesn't convert its credits/points/meals into dollar value.

GRADUATE, ANTHROPOLOGY, ARIZONA STATE UNIVERSITY

Keep a large supply of TUMS® on hand at all times.

SENIOR, PSYCHOLOGY, STATE UNIVERSITY OF NEW YORK—BUFFALO

Although the food might seem good at first, when it is served in such A PREDICTABLE AND UNCHANGING ROTATION, it gets old very quickly.

JUNIOR, COGNITIVE SCIENCE, UNIVERSITY OF VIRGINIA

When you find something that you like, don't eat it all the time—you'll get sick of it!

SENIOR, BIOLOGY, TOWSON UNIVERSITY

I was gonna make sure I was **getting my money's worth**. I think Dining Services lost money on me—I ate like a horse. I also made friends with some of the ladies behind the counter, and they hooked me up with large portions.

SENIOR, BIOLOGY, COLLEGE OF WILLIAM & MARY

The food is **not all that bad** and hey . . . I already paid for it, so I might as well eat it.

GRADUATE, PSYCHOLOGY, SYRACUSE UNIVERSITY

It beats COOKING FOR YOURSELF.

GRADUATE, AMERICAN CIVILIZATIONS, BROWN UNIVERSITY

WEIGHT WATCHING

I would come to the dining hall, see that the food was bad—but still eat some of it—then go back to my room still hungry and order a pizza or Chinese food. That was not a good idea. I definitely put on

the freshman fifteen.

GRADUATE, NEUROSCIENCE AND BEHAVIOR, WESLEYAN UNIVERSITY

DINING HALL FOOD IS FATTENING! Eat a balanced meal (yes, including vegetables!) and drink orange juice or milk instead of pop.

SENIOR, PRE-MEDICINE/PSYCHOLOGY, UNIVERSITY OF IOWA

The freshman fifteen can go either way. The food sucked so **I lost fifteen pounds!**

GRADUATE, BIOLOGY, CLEMSON UNIVERSITY

I quickly learned that I needed to VARY MY FOODS: McDonald's three times a week wasn't going to be healthy.

GRADUATE, SOCIOLOGY/FAMILY STUDIES AND HUMAN DEVELOPMENT, UNIVERSITY OF ARIZONA

You MUST monitor your food intake! They'll let you eat till you pop, and you will! Be mindful of your eating habits—too many people make themselves miserable because they are not attentive and then they're shocked by their reflection or their parents' reactions when they go home for the holidays.

GRADUATE, PSYCHOLOGY, XAVIER UNIVERSITY

TAKE IT WITH YOU

Load up on **hard-boiled eggs** to take to your room for when hunger sets in later.

GRADUATE, POLITICAL SCIENCE, FLORIDA INTERNATIONAL UNIVERSITY

It is a good idea to keep SOME SPARE SNACKS in your room for when dinner is not edible.

GRADUATE, GOVERNMENT, COLLEGE OF WILLIAM & MARY

Bring Tupperware® and "steal" the cereal and fruit and bread. (It's not really stealing is it? Technically you did PAY for it . . . right!?)

SENIOR, BIOLOGY, OBERLIN COLLEGE

Take **fruits** out of the dining hall because you are going to be hungry late at night.

GRADUATE, ZOOLOGY, CONNECTICUT COLLEGE

DINING DOS AND DON'TS

MYSTERY MEAT AND OTHER CULINARY PERILS

I quickly learned to steer clear of anything with "MEDLEY," "HASH," OR "CASSEROLE" in the name.

SENIOR, BIOLOGY, OBERLIN COLLEGE

Be very careful of the meat they serve later in the week. Monday's meatloaf has a strange way of reappearing in Friday's spaghetti sauce.

JUNIOR, ENGLISH, GEORGETOWN UNIVERSITY

Don't eat anything you can't readily identify.

JUNIOR, NEUROSCIENCE, UNIVERSITY OF PITTSBURGH

A box of **instant noodles** is a must!

JUNIOR, BIOLOGY, STATE UNIVERSITY OF NEW YORK—BINGHAMTON

Chef Boyardee really knows what he is doing.

GRADUATE, BIOCHEMISTRY/SPANISH, UNIVERSITY OF WISCONSIN—MADISON

Check the school newspaper; there is always **something offered for free** in terms of food.

SENIOR, ANTHROPOLOGY/INTERNATIONAL STUDIES, NORTHWESTERN UNIVERSITY

I quickly learned how to make my own creations; it's amazing how much can be done with dining hall food.

SENIOR, RHETORIC AND COMMUNICATION STUDIES, UNIVERSITY OF RICHMOND

You can make your own **pizza bagels** with pasta sauce and cheese!

SENIOR, COMMUNICATIONS, UNIVERSITY OF CALIFORNIA—SANTA BARBARA

Quosadillas with spaghetti sauce are delicious.

JUNIOR, PHILOSOPHY, NORTHWESTERN UNIVERSITY

I learned that if you poured clam chowder on top of spaghetti you got SEAFOOD FETTUCINE ALFREDO.

GRADUATE, PSYCHOLOGY, UNIVERSITY OF CALIFORNIA—SAN DIEGO

DINING DOS AND DON'TS

It's really hard to control yourself when you're offered ice cream 24/7!

SENIOR, CHEMISTRY, CORNELL UNIVERSITY

To exercise lots.

SENIOR, LINGUISTICS, BRIGHAM YOUNG UNIVERSITY

My mom is an amazing cook.

SENIOR, EXERCISE AND MOVEMENT SCIENCE, UNIVERSITY OF OREGON

The freshman fifteen is directly related to the all-you-can-eat buffet and dessert bar.

GRADUATE, ENGLISH/MUSIC, THE COLLEGE OF WILLIAM & MARY

What it's like to have food poisoning NIGHTLY.

GRADUATE, HISTORY, UNIVERSITY OF MASSACHUSETTS

That anything tastes better with salt.

SENIOR, PRE-LAW, UNIVERSITY OF ILLINOIS—URBANA-CHAMPAIGN

SENIOR, SOCIOLOGY, COLGATE COLLEGE

chapter

15

SPRING BREAK/ GOING ABROAD

A good guidebook does wonders.

SENIOR, SOCIOLOGY, COLGATE COLLEGE

A BROAD EXPERIENCE

I TRAVELED TO RUSSIA to work in orphanages with some people from my department; it changed my life. I would suggest that everyone travel abroad if they can.

GRADUATE, SPEECH-LANGUAGE PATHOLOGY, TOWSON UNIVERSITY

My most memorable experience was the summer I spent abroad. I worked for two months, first in London, completely on my own, and then I studied through a school program at Oxford University. The entire experience was absolutely invaluable; I matured and grew in more ways than I could possibly have foreseen. And a big part of that was just getting far away from everyone and everything that was familiar to me.

GRADUATE, PSYCHOLOGY, UNIVERSITY OF TEXAS—AUSTIN

If you spend a semester on another continent like Europe, make sure you travel to as many countries as possible during your time there. When will you get another chance to have a home base so close to so many new experiences?

GRADUATE, ENGLISH, PRINCETON UNIVERSITY

The thought of moving to another continent might sound scary, but this is the only time in your life when **you'll be able to just pick up and go**. Don't waste the opportunity.

GRADUATE, GOVERNMENT, CONNECTICUT COLLEGE

GO TO A PLACE WHERE YOU ARE FLUENT in the language so that you can fully immerse yourself in the culture.

GRADUATE, BIOLOGY, EMORY UNIVERSITY

If you're worried about the cost of going abroad, there are special loans for this kind of thing. Check with your abroad office to see what your school offers.

SOPHOMORE, MECHANICAL ENGINEERING, UNIVERSITY OF EVANSVILLE

SPRING BREAK: THE FINE PRINT

A couple of my classmates were **stranded in Mexico** because the travel agency "forgot" to mention that in the fine print it says that only the airfare TO Mexico was included in the price, not the airfare FROM Mexico.

JUNIOR, HISTORY/PRE-LAW, OHIO STATE UNIVERSITY

There was this five-day, four-night get-away to Cancun, for $199. All you had to do was buy a plane ticket, put down a $1,000 security deposit, and supply your own food. Well, the room was left in "unsatisfactory" condition, and **my buddies and I lost our deposit**.

SOPHOMORE, BIOLOGICAL SCIENCE, FLORIDA STATE UNIVERSITY

HOW TO GET SPRING BREAK DEALS

If it is a package deal, try to find someone that has used/done that one before. It is easy to find people to recommend the best hotels, hot spots, and restaurants if they have been there before.

GRADUATE, INTERNATIONAL BUSINESS, UNIVERSITY OF TEXAS—AUSTIN

BE WARY OF PACKAGE DEALS. The people who offer the deals are usually third party and tack their expense into the package. Cut out the middleman and deal directly with the hotels or find a place like priceline.com

SOPHOMORE, ECONOMICS, UNIVERSITY OF TEXAS—AUSTIN

Don't go on spring break with people at school whom you find annoying. **If they annoy you at school,** they'll annoy you five times as much on the beaches of the Bahamas.

SENIOR, COMMUNICATIONS, CORNELL UNIVERSITY

If you don't have the money to go away for spring break, **road trips with your friends** always wind up being a good time no matter where you go.

JUNIOR, BUSINESS, KETTERING UNIVERSITY

When you are a freshman or sophomore, go to the usual spring break spots like Cancun and go crazy. But once you get a little older, realize that there is a whole world out there to explore during spring break—not just places that serve two-for-one tequila shots.

SENIOR, JOURNALISM, UNIVERSITY OF FLORIDA

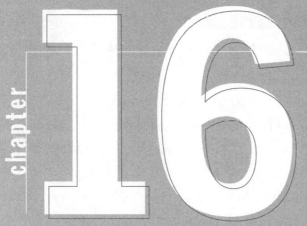

16

MONEY MANAGEMENT

It's simple. Don't spend what you don't have.

GRADUATE, ENGLISH, MOREHOUSE COLLEGE

Just know that there's a difference between "WANTS" and "NEEDS."

SENIOR, CRIMINAL JUSTICE, UNIVERSITY OF MARYLAND—COLLEGE PARK

Don't blow your financial aid money on anything but school and books; if you have money left over, save it until the end of the semester when you know you'll get another check for the next semester, and either spend it then or put it in a savings account.

SENIOR, JOURNALISM, UNIVERSITY OF TEXAS—AUSTIN

Have fun, but never at the expense of your necessities. NEVER LEAVE YOUR BANK ACCOUNT EMPTY.

GRADUATE, ENGLISH, GEORGIA STATE UNIVERSITY

Don't charge anything that you couldn't pay for right then and there from your checking account. Keep money for food and spending money in two separate accounts.

SENIOR, BIOLOGY, BUCKNELL UNIVERSITY

Sales are good. Look for them. Checking accounts are good. Get one, but don't forget to balance your checkbook.

JUNIOR, PHILOSOPHY, NORTHWESTERN UNIVERSITY

Keep a twenty-dollar bill in your pocket. It's easy to spend twenty bucks if you have singles and five-dollar bills, but breaking that twenty is a lot harder to do.

GRADUATE, CHEMICAL ENGINEERING, UNIVERSITY OF VIRGINIA

Take out a certain amount of money each week and don't take out any more. If you do that **your money will last longer**, plus you won't keep getting charged all of those ATM fees.

SENIOR, PSYCHOLOGY, HAMPTON UNIVERSITY

Balance your checkbook so that you see how often you are **withdrawing money from the ATM**. Those $20 withdrawals add up quickly.

JUNIOR, MICROBIOLOGY AND CELL SCIENCE, UNIVERSITY OF FLORIDA

If you have a set budget, you need to BE AWARE AND PLAN ACCORDINGLY. You can't order pizza every night if you only have $200 to spend for the next five months.

SENIOR, LEGAL STUDIES, QUINNIPIAC UNIVERSITY

I use a debit card, **not a credit card** so I can't overdraw. Also, save the shopping trips for when you go home to your parents or after taking a big exam.

SENIOR, ENGLISH/PSYCHOLOGY, UNIVERSITY OF MICHIGAN—ANN ARBOR

SET A BUDGET FOR YOURSELF, try to limit extraneous expenses, and do not hesitate to tell your girlfriend that you can't always buy dinner.

GRADUATE, POLITICAL SCIENCE, UNIVERSITY OF FLORIDA

Stick with **one guilty pleasure** that you can waste money on! CDs, shoes, concerts, what have you . . . but try to discipline yourself to one thing.

GRADUATE, ETHNIC STUDIES/HISTORY, BROWN UNIVERSITY

THE DEVIL IN DISGUISE

DO NOT get a credit card. I have never had a credit card and I have made it through four years of college just fine. I have so many friends who ran up their credit card bills and now have problems paying off the charges and the interest.

GRADUATE, BUSINESS ADMINISTRATION, UNIVERSITY OF MISSOURI—COLUMBIA

Credit card debt REALLY is a big deal! I racked up so much debt and I didn't even realize it. A piece of plastic lets you use more money faster, so be careful with it. **Budget your money!**

SENIOR, CHEMISTRY, CORNELL UNIVERSITY

Get a credit card and don't use it. Or, if you do, only spend money that you have. It's time to start building credit now. But don't spend money you don't have. I know people who had to drop out of school to pay off debts.

SENIOR, LINGUISTICS, BRIGHAM YOUNG UNIVERSITY

PAY OFF YOUR CREDIT CARD BILL IN FULL EVERY MONTH. If you don't trust yourself not to splurge, use it only for gasoline for your car or something like that. Doing so will build outstanding credit so that when you graduate you can take loans from the bank more easily for "real world' things.

SENIOR, BIOLOGY/ENVIRONMENTAL STUDIES, WASHINGTON COLLEGE

Ask the credit card company for a $1,000 **spending limit**. That way, you can't go over $1,000, even if you want to.

SENIOR, BIOLOGY, WAKE FOREST UNIVERSITY

Get a part-time job. You appreciate your money when you can translate a dollar into how long you'd have to work to get it.

GRADUATE, ENGLISH, CORNELL UNIVERSITY

Find a good summer job and **save as much money as you can** for unexpected expenses.

SENIOR, ACCOUNTING, UTAH STATE UNIVERSITY

ONCE UPON A CAMPUS

177

CHECK THE INTERNET for scholarships, there are a lot out there.

GRADUATE, ZOOLOGY, CONNECTICUT COLLEGE

Scholarships are definitely the way to go; one would be surprised at how much money there is for students, just waiting to be asked for.

GRADUATE, ENGLISH, UNIVERSITY OF FLORIDA

Try to get scholarships—there is one for everybody. In fact, Joe Smith from Yourtown, USA, can probably **find a specialized scholarship** for a trumpet player interested in attending Beefcake College.

GRADUATE, PSYCHOLOGY, EAST TENNESSEE STATE UNIVERSITY

There is **always free food** around. Go to meetings that offer free dinner or treats.

GRADUATE, MATH, CARLETON COLLEGE

Buy food and make it whenever you can. Make a big meal on Sunday and **eat leftovers**. Get a membership at a Sam's Club or Costco.

SENIOR, GOVERNMENT, UNIVERSITY OF VIRGINIA

Always EAT ON YOUR MEAL PLAN unless it's a special occasion.

SENIOR, ENGLISH/PSYCHOLOGY, UNIVERSITY OF MICHIGAN—ANN ARBOR

Learn how to cook! It can be a good way to get your mind off things and save money. It is also a lot healthier than eating out. Invite friends over and offer to cook in exchange for them doing the clean up.

GRADUATE, BIOCHEMISTRY, UNIVERSITY OF CALIFORNIA—DAVIS

Wendy's is known for their 99-cent menu and it will become one of your best friends. It can make at least THREE MEALS OUT OF TEN DOLLARS.

GRADUATE, BUSINESS ADMINISTRATION, FLORIDA A&M UNIVERSITY

One sign that you are overdoing it is when the delivery guy calls you by your first name.

GRADUATE, SOCIAL RELATIONS, JAMES MADISON COLLEGE AT MICHIGAN STATE UNIVERSITY

Live off of Ramen Noodles, the ultimate cheap college feast.

GRADUATE, PSYCHOLOGY, EAST TENNESSEE STATE UNIVERSITY

TRICKS OF THE TRADE

SHOP CONSIGNMENT! Learn about all the free perks on campus and cheap discounts you get as a student. Most airlines, restaurants, etc. offer a discount to college students if you show an ID.

SENIOR, JOURNALISM, UNIVERSITY OF TEXAS—AUSTIN

Shop at the dollar store, at garage sales, and on eBay.

SENIOR, LINGUISTICS, BRIGHAM YOUNG UNIVERSITY

Clip coupons and find free things to do with friends.

SENIOR, BIOLOGY, BUCKNELL UNIVERSITY

You'd be amazed at what you can find by **asking around in your dorm** instead of going out and buying it (i.e. printer paper, even some furniture!).

JUNIOR, SCIENCE PRE-PROFESSIONAL, UNIVERSITY OF NOTRE DAME

Don't buy a bunch of new stuff before you go to college. You don't know what the fashion is going to be or what you'll need. You'll buy capris and everyone will be wearing bell-bottoms. Or you'll buy a new toaster and realize the dorm has one and you didn't need It.

JUNIOR, COMPUTER SCIENCE, UNIVERSITY OF CHICAGO

17

SAFETY

Common sense is the key to keeping yourself and your belongings safe.

SENIOR, POLITICAL SCIENCE, UNIVERSITY OF
CALIFORNIA—SAN DIEGO

THE KEY TO SECURITY

Although you should be open to new ideas and people, your room shouldn't. **Always lock** it when you're not there.

SENIOR, LEGAL STUDIES, QUINNIPIAC UNIVERSITY

Lock your door, and threaten your roommate if she doesn't lock the door.

GRADUATE, ENGINEERING SCIENCES, DARTMOUTH COLLEGE

ALWAYS LOCK YOUR DOOR when you are away or sleeping. I can't even tell you how many stories I've heard about drunk people accidentally walking into the wrong room late at night.

GRADUATE, COGNITIVE SCIENCE, UNIVERSITY OF VIRGINIA

SAFETY

Carry **pepper spray** in your hand; it doesn't do you any good in your backpack.

GRADUATE, PSYCHOLOGY, UNIVERSITY OF ILLINOIS—URBANA-CHAMPAIGN

Don't go jogging at night, especially not while wearing headphones. There are twenty-four hours in a day, twelve of which are daylight—jog then and stay safe.

SENIOR, GOVERNMENT, UNIVERSITY OF VIRGINIA

ONCE UPON A CAMPUS

Carry mace if you're out alone at night a lot and call a friend while walking home so that if something were to happen, someone would know you were missing, where you were, and when it happened.

SENIOR, POLITICAL SCIENCE, UNIVERSITY OF CALIFORNIA—DAVIS

Never put yourself in a situation where **no one knows where you are**. If you didn't come home, how long would it be before anyone noticed?

GRADUATE, PSYCHOLOGY, UNIVERSITY OF ALABAMA

BETTER SAFE THAN SORRY

Be aware of the people around you at all times. Most campuses have police who will escort you on campus. Use this service if you feel the slightest concern for your safety. **Get a cell phone** and know their number and the number for roadside assistance.

GRADUATE, ENGLISH, TEXAS WOMEN'S UNIVERSITY

Always be conscious of the fact that people may be at the school for more than just education. Keeping an eye on your stuff and LOCKING YOUR BIKE SECURELY is not paranoia.

GRADUATE, POLITICAL SCIENCE, UNIVERSITY OF FLORIDA

Use the buddy system. It's always better to **walk with a friend** than wander by yourself.

SENIOR, POLITICAL SCIENCE, UNIVERSITY OF WASHINGTON

Never walk home by yourself at night if you are intoxicated (drunk or high); should something happen, you may not be in the right frame of mind to handle it. Don't let people who have been drinking drive you ANYWHERE—just call the shuttle or cab!

SENIOR, BIOLOGY, OBERLIN COLLEGE

Try not to get so drunk that you are **UNABLE TO PROTECT YOURSELF**, and if you do get that drunk, make sure you are with friends you can trust.

GRADUATE, GOVERNMENT, DARTMOUTH COLLEGE

Never take an open drink from someone you don't know.

SENIOR, POLITICAL SCIENCE, UNIVERSITY OF MASSACHUSETTS—AMHERST

WHO CAN YOU TRUST?

Don't think you really know someone because you've hung out with them for a month. TRUST IS SOMETHING THAT'S EARNED over a long period of time.

SENIOR, PSYCHOLOGY, HAMPTON UNIVERSITY

A girl should know a guy before she lets him come to her house, and she should always meet him in a public setting for the first couple of dates.

SENIOR, JOURNALISM, UNIVERSITY OF TEXAS—AUSTIN

Know your dorm neighbors so if you see someone who shouldn't be there, they will stand out and look suspicious.

SENIOR, POLITICAL SCIENCE, UNIVERSITY OF NORTH TEXAS

Mark your name on EVERYTHING!

GRADUATE, EXERCISE PHYSIOLOGY/MEDICINE, BRIGHAM YOUNG UNIVERSITY

Don't leave your stuff lying around. As much as you'd like to believe that no one wants your biochemistry book, you'd be surprised—there are weirdos out there.

GRADUATE, PSYCHOLOGY/ORGANIZATIONAL STUDIES, UNIVERSITY OF MICHIGAN—ANN ARBOR

VISIT CAMPUS SECURITY to see what advice they have. For example, our security office has this software program that can track your laptop if it gets stolen.

GRADUATE, BIOCHEMISTRY/SPANISH, UNIVERSITY OF WISCONSIN—MADISON

SAFETY

Don't bring too much expensive stuff to college. Make sure that everything you really care about is kept in a secure place and that the rest can be replaced easily.

GRADUATE, POLITICAL SCIENCE, UNIVERSITY OF CALIFORNIA—SAN DIEGO

BUY A TRUNK OR SAFE BOX so you can keep money, jewelry, and expensive stuff locked up. Establish rules with your living buddies about who visits and under what supervision.

SENIOR, SOCIAL WORK, NIAGARA UNIVERSITY

Use common sense with your belongings. You may trust your roommate, but can you say that about her friends who may come into your room?

JUNIOR, MICROBIOLOGY/CELL SCIENCE, UNIVERSITY OF FLORIDA

Carry a big backpack. Having a small backpack may force you to carry some of your books or belongings by hand. If you do that, it will be easier to misplace or lose something. You should be able to fit everything you need in your bag, because there are no lockers in college.

SENIOR, PSYCHOLOGY/SOCIAL BEHAVIOR, UNIVERSITY OF CALIFORNIA—IRVINE

I had a little CAMPBELL'S SOUP CAN that I used to secretly store valuables, which I kept in my underwear drawer.

GRADUATE, SOCIOLOGY/FAMILY STUDIES AND HUMAN DEVELOPMENT, UNIVERSITY OF ARIZONA

Keep your stuff WITH YOU when you are in the library; so many people get their bags stolen.

SENIOR, BIOLOGY, OBERLIN COLLEGE

Don't boast about your new tech gadgets—that's the most obvious invite for losing your stuff.

GRADUATE, SOCIOLOGY, UNIVERSITY OF CALIFORNIA—IRVINE

Don't keep **expensive things** out in broad daylight.

JUNIOR, BIOLOGY, ARIZONA STATE UNIVERSITY

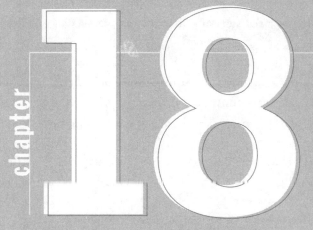

PREPARING FOR THE FUTURE

I always thought that when you were a senior, recruiters flocked to your door and begged you to sign on for a position at some company relating exactly to your major. Apparently, that's not what happens.

GRADUATE, BIOLOGY,
UNIVERSITY OF CENTRAL FLORIDA

CRAFTING THE PERFECT RESUME

I WAS OVER-PREPARED FOR THE JOB MARKET. I had internships during my summer and January breaks. I also completed a senior thesis and attended conferences so that I had completed a major piece of writing and had presentation experience.

GRADUATE, ENVIRONMENTAL SCIENCE AND POLICY VALUES, WELLS COLLEGE

I wish I had done a better internship during my senior year or summer breaks. Internships help you figure out what jobs are out there and what you need to know to get them.

GRADUATE, ENVIRONMENTAL STUDIES, EMORY AND HENRY COLLEGE

GET GOOD INTERNSHIPS! This is the only time you will be given responsibility without having any experience. Employers and graduate schools will look favorably on these internships.

GRADUATE, POLITICAL SCIENCE, UNIVERSITY OF CALIFORNIA—SAN DIEGO

I wish I hadn't concentrated so much on getting involved in **extracurricular activities to pad my resume**; it ended up costing me a better GPA.

GRADUATE, BIOLOGY, COLLEGE OF CHARLESTON

I wish that I had gotten A MINOR IN SPANISH. Being able to speak two languages makes you a better commodity in the job market.

GRADUATE, CRIMINAL JUSTICE, WESTCHESTER UNIVERSITY

Employers and grad schools want to work with people who show some level of focus, not people who dabble in a little bit of everything.

GRADUATE, MARKETING, HOWARD UNIVERSITY

If you think there's a chance you're going to go to graduate school, MAKING ACADEMIC CONTACTS early becomes important, especially when the time comes for you to get recommendations.

GRADUATE, SPANISH, LOYOLA COLLEGE

Employers want to know what your experience is, not what grades you got. Graduate school is a balance between the two. They want to know that you challenged yourself with the classes you picked and that you participated in something besides school.

GRADUATE, CRIMINOLOGY/LAW AND SOCIETY, UNIVERSITY OF CALIFORNIA—IRVINE

I wish I had networked more with alumni and attended graduate school workshops put on by the university.

GRADUATE, POLITICAL ECONOMY OF INDUSTRIAL SOCIETIES, UNIVERSITY OF CALIFORNIA—BERKELEY

I should have taken advantage of **the mock interview sessions** offered by the career center.

GRADUATE, ART AND DESIGN, LAGRANGE COLLEGE

I wish I had attended more **optional lectures** about applying to graduate schools.

GRADUATE, CLARINET PERFORMANCE, VASSAR COLLEGE

I wish I had taken advantage of THE CAREER CENTER. I would have been exposed to more companies and had more opportunities to practice interviews.

GRADUATE, MICROBIOLOGY, INDIANA UNIVERSITY

I wish I had taken a class on writing resumés and cover letters, job strategies, and interviewing skills. I graduated thinking I would have no problem getting a job, but it's a lot harder than I thought—I wish someone had prepared me better for that reality.

GRADUATE, CRIMINAL JUSTICE, VITERBO UNIVERSITY

I should have studied the job market more carefully and found out what exactly it is that I wanted to do. I should have taken advantage of alumni networking and professors to talk about what certain jobs are like.

GRADUATE, INTERNATIONAL STUDIES, BRIGHAM YOUNG UNIVERSITY

I wish I had known **what classes would be best** to take for my major and the career I wanted to go into.

GRADUATE, BIOLOGY, CLEMSON UNIVERSITY

I wish I had taken the GRE waaaaay earlier. I should have TAKEN A PREP CLASS back in the early part of my junior year. I'm currently jobless and frantically applying to grad schools.

GRADUATE, PSYCHOLOGY/ORGANIZATIONAL STUDIES, UNIVERSITY OF MICHIGAN—ANN ARBOR

I wich I had worked hard all four years. It is tough to change your GPA drastically. It seems to go down more quickly than it goes up.

GRADUATE, POLITICAL SCIENCE/SOCIOLOGY/LEGAL STUDIES, UNIVERSITY OF WISCONSIN—MADISON

Studying more would have helped me. I have a 3.6 GPA, and there is no reason why it shouldn't have been a 3.9.

GRADUATE, BIOCHEMISTRY/SPANISH, UNIVERSITY OF WISCONSIN—MADISON

GET YOUR RECOMMENDATIONS right after you finish a course with a professor, as opposed to senior year when you need them. That way, you're fresh in their minds.

GRADUATE, PSYCHOLOGY, CONNECTICUT COLLEGE

I took college seriously, and I got into law school and I landed a great job. The people who thought college was something they did not have to work at are still looking for a job and did not make it to graduate school.

GRADUATE, CRIMINOLOGY/LAW AND SOCIETY, UNIVERSITY OF CALIFORNIA—IRVINE

THE DEAN OF STUDENT LIFE OR ACADEMIC AFFAIRS. And more importantly—his or her assistant. They can often tip you off to job opportunities on and off campus.

DEPARTMENT SECRETARIES IN YOUR MAJOR. They also can help you find part-time work.

A MEMBER OF THE FACULTY WHO WILL MENTOR YOU. Find a professor whose field of study you're interested in or you think, based on a certain interaction you have with her, is really high-energy.

THE FOLKS IN THE CAREER SERVICE OFFICE. That's a great place to try and look for a part-time job as a freshman. By the time you're a senior they'll know you and like you. They'll go out of their way to help you if they know you.

19 STRESS RELIEVERS

A good night's sleep can work miracles.

GRADUATE, ENGINEERING SCIENCES,
DARTMOUTH COLLEGE

Cleaning. Oddly enough, my favorite time to clean was when I had big assignments due.

GRADUATE, PUBLIC RELATIONS, UNIVERSITY OF GEORGIA

EXERCISING...plus it kept off the freshman fifteen.

GRADUATE, BIOLOGICAL SCIENCES, SOUTHERN ILLINOIS UNIVERSITY—EDWARDSVILLE

Even **socializing at the library** during study breaks helps a lot!

SENIOR, POLITICAL SCIENCE, UNIVERSITY OF NORTH FLORIDA

Having water fights in the hall, watching "Wedding Story" on TLC, and playing in the snow.

GRADUATE, BIOLOGY, MIDLAND LUTHERAN COLLEGE

Going to Dunkin' Donuts or to **the movies**.

GRADUATE, BIOLOGY, THE COLLEGE OF NEW JERSEY

Going to the coffee house for a cup of coffee and chatting with friends, or playing guitar and writing songs with my friends.

SENIOR, MUSIC/ECONOMICS, LAKE FOREST COLLEGE

Looking up professors on COMPUTER SEARCH ENGINES to find dirt on them.

SENIOR, BIOLOGY/NEUROSCIENCE/PSYCHOLOGY, BRANDEIS UNIVERSITY

Long walks through the safe neighborhoods around campus. You get to dabble in the old family-centered life you miss and you get to free your mind from the worries that surround you when you're on campus.

GRADUATE, PSYCHOLOGY, XAVIER UNIVERSITY

I loved to **lay around in the grass** under a tree on a nice sunny day. It's the best way to get your mind off those challenging assignments that lie ahead.

SENIOR, PSYCHOLOGY, UNIVERSITY OF MARYLAND—COLLEGE PARK

Watching soap operas. I even went so far as to plan one semester so no classes would interfere with my favorite soap!

SENIOR, LEGAL STUDIES, QUINNIPIAC UNIVERSITY

Video games are a great way to work out your aggressions.

GRADUATE, MICROBIOLOGY, INDIANA UNIVERSITY

Emailing friends.

JUNIOR, MICROBIOLOGY AND CELL SCIENCE, UNIVERSITY OF FLORIDA

DOWNLOADING MUSIC onto the computer and searching the Web for useless things.

GRADUATE, BIOLOGY/ENGLISH, INDIANA UNIVERSITY—BLOOMINGTON

Daydreaming over your chemistry textbook.

GRADUATE, MATH, CARLETON COLLEGE

ONCE UPON A CAMPUS

20

EMBARRASSING MOMENTS

College is nothing but a list of embarrassing experiences. Get ready to enjoy them all!

SENIOR, POLITICAL SCIENCE, INDIANA UNIVERSITY

A "CLOTHES" ENCOUNTER

My most embarrassing moment was coming home on New Year's Eve and having my roommate inform me that MY SHINY SILVER PANTS HAD A HUGE RIP in the butt. I had been out all night like that!

SENIOR, PRE-LAW, UNIVERSITY OF ILLINOIS—URBANA-CHAMPAIGN

I got caught streaking by a police officer . . . he let me go, though.

SENIOR, PSYCHOLOGY, UNIVERSITY OF VIRGINIA

For crew initiation I had to wear the same outfit for a whole week and then **sing and dance in the cafeteria!**

GRADUATE, BIOLOGY, GEORGETOWN UNIVERSITY

AN ACCIDENTAL AUDIENCE

I slipped on some ice on the sidewalk in front of about 200 people, all gathered together because they knew about the ice patch and were waiting for people to slip.

SENIOR, LINGUISTICS, BRIGHAM YOUNG UNIVERSITY

One night at a party, some friends convinced a girl I had never laid eyes on before that I was in love with her. Needless to say, WHEN SHE CONFRONTED ME about it in front of a bunch of people, I wanted to crawl into a hole.

GRADUATE, HISTORY, UNIVERSITY OF MASSACHUSETTS

I was showing a group of students and their parents around campus and **I slipped and fell down a massive flight of wet stairs**. Afterward, I triumphantly got up and yelled 'I'M OKAY!' Nevertheless, it was embarrassing.

SENIOR, GENDER STUDIES/RELIGIOUS STUDIES, BROWN UNIVERSITY

I accidentally pulled out a plug in a public computer room and every computer was shut down. It happened before final exams, when papers were due!

SENIOR, BIOLOGY, STATE UNIVERSITY OF NEW YORK—BUFFALO

My freshman year, I was at a party during the winter and tripped headlong **into a swimming pool**. Mind you, I was sober.

SENIOR, GOVERNMENT, UNIVERSITY OF TEXAS—AUSTIN

I PASSED OUT during a fire drill and had to be carried upstairs when it was over.

SENIOR, NEUROSCIENCE, UNIVERSITY OF ROCHESTER

My most embarrassing experience was when I realized how thin the walls are in the dorms and that everyone could hear me singing in my room.

GRADUATE, BIOCHEMISTRY/SPANISH, UNIVERSITY OF WISCONSIN—MADISON

NOT-SO-CLASSY CLASSROOM MISHAPS

First day of classes. Freshman year. A seventy-five-person lecture. **I tipped over in my desk** as I was reaching for my pen. Everyone, including the professor, laughed at me.

GRADUATE, CHEMICAL ENGINEERING, UNIVERSITY OF VIRGINIA

The lab gloves in my basic chemistry class were slippery and I dropped a bottle, sending a very strong base flying everywhere. They called the fire department and made me stand in the chemical shower in the middle of class! When they finally took me to the ER, they said I was fine and released me. But I made that evening's news!

SENIOR, EVOLUTION/ECOLOGY, UNIVERSITY OF CALIFORNIA—DAVIS

I meant to send a romantic email to my boyfriend and **accidentally sent it** to a professor instead. (The professor's email address was listed underneath my boyfriend's in my email address book.) I got an "A" in the class!

GRADUATE, HISTORY, RUTGERS UNIVERSITY

I sat in the wrong classroom for about 20 minutes before realizing it was a graduate class and then I made a not-so-nonchalant exit.

GRADUATE, ENGLISH/AMERICAN STUDIES, UNIVERSITY OF NOTRE DAME

I got **food poisoning** on my first college date.

SENIOR, BIOLOGY, BUCKNELL UNIVERSITY

A BIRD POOPED ON MY LEG during orientation week. It was the first time I had met anyone at school and for the rest of the week everyone knew me as the girl the bird pooped on.

JUNIOR, BIOMEDICAL ENGINEERING, SAINT LOUIS UNIVERSITY

I fell asleep in my friends' room, and they put a large plastic rooster head in bed next to me and took a large color photo.

GRADUATE, ENGLISH/FRENCH, CORNELL UNIVERSITY

I walked in on my roommate not once, not twice, but three times when she was naked with her boyfriend. She didn't have a signal system.

SENIOR, BIOCHEMISTRY AND ENGLISH, UNIVERSITY OF CALIFORNIA—DAVIS

Sometimes you just gotta take it and **not be embarrassed**. It makes life a lot easier.

GRADUATE, PHYSICS, GROSSMONT COLLEGE

Hey, it's college. NOTHING is embarrassing.

GRADUATE, BIOLOGY, SPRING HILL COLLEGE

FONDEST MEMORIES AND BIGGEST REGRETS

I didn't have enough fun while I was in college. I found the perfect balance of work and play too late. Find it early!

GRADUATE, PSYCHOLOGY, UNIVERSITY OF GEORGIA

GOOD TIMES

A group of us **burned our notes** from our Genetics class after a miserable semester. It was good riddance and a great stress reliever.

SENIOR, BIOLOGY/ENVIRONMENTAL STUDIES, WASHINGTON COLLEGE

Last year I lived in an on-campus apartment with two other girls. We, along with the people in the apartment next to us, threw A MARDI GRAS PARTY. We handed out flyers all over campus. The place was so packed that you couldn't move, and the cops broke it up within the first hour. It was quite a success for those few minutes, though!

JUNIOR, BIOLOGY, COLLEGE OF WILLIAM & MARY

Road trips are great. I'll never forget all the road trips I've taken with different girlfriends at college—Omaha, Twin Cities, little hick towns with divey bars. It's all been a blast.

SENIOR, BIOCHEMISTRY AND MOLECULAR BIOLOGY, CORNELL COLLEGE

FONDEST MEMORIES AND BIGGEST REGRETS

We don't get much snow in Cincinnati, but during the winter of my sophomore year we had a big storm. I was the resident assistant for our basketball team and many of them were out-of-towners who had never seen snow. We all bundled up, went outside, and started **an enormous snowball fight** along with the residents of the dorm next door. It was great!

GRADUATE, PSYCHOLOGY, XAVIER UNIVERSITY

My most memorable experience was **rallying on campus** against violence toward women. It was so cool walking through the campus chanting for women's rights.

GRADUATE, ENGLISH, GEORGE MASON UNIVERSITY

My most memorable experience was **getting a 4.0 GPA** for a semester. I had never done that in high school and it was one of my goals.

JUNIOR, ACCOUNTING/FINANCE, WASHINGTON UNIVERSITY—ST. LOUIS

I passed a test for which I had studied for two weeks straight. It was a big deal because the test was given by a professor who was notorious for his detailed tests. I felt great and I learned what I was capable of doing.

GRADUATE, ENGLISH, MOREHOUSE COLLEGE

WINDING UP WITH A BANG

My most memorable experience was the day **I finished up my last term paper** and handed it to my professor. As I put it in his hands he said to me very calmly, "You are now a graduate."

GRADUATE, SOCIOLOGY/POLITICAL SCIENCE, STATE UNIVERSITY OF NEW YORK—BUFFALO

At graduation I was HONORED WITH AN AWARD named after a late professor who meant the world to me.

GRADUATE, ENVIRONMENTAL POLICY, SCIENCE, AND VALUES, WELLS COLLEGE

My most memorable moment was walking out of my last exam my senior year. It was bittersweet. I wanted to stay because I loved the life . . . but I knew it was time to move on, and I was proud of what I had done.

GRADUATE, HISTORY, UNIVERSITY OF MASSACHUSETTS

KNOW A GOOD THING WHEN YOU HAVE IT

I regret that I only truly **enjoyed my last year of college**. I appreciated where I was and who I was with only when I knew it wasn't going to last.

GRADUATE, COGNITIVE SCIENCE, UNIVERSITY OF VIRGINIA

My biggest regret is that I didn't take advantage of more FREE CONCERTS, SPEECHES, and EVENTS.

GRADUATE, BIOLOGY, INDIANA UNIVERSITY

I regret not taking advantage of **everything college had to offer**. There were so many speakers and colloquiums, but I was always too busy or too tired. I wish I'd experienced more of the diversity and intellectual environment.

SENIOR, NEUROSCIENCE, UNIVERSITY OF ROCHESTER

My biggest regret is not having **more social time**. I was always a "study freak."

SENIOR, BUSINESS/SPEECH COMMUNICATIONS, HOUSTON BAPTIST UNIVERSITY

My biggest regret is blowing off fun plans in order to get work done. Yes, schoolwork is very important, but there are A LOT OF OTHER EXPERIENCES at college that will stay with you forever.

SENIOR, GOVERNMENT, UNIVERSITY OF VIRGINIA

JUMP RIGHT IN!

My biggest regret was GETTING TIED DOWN WITH A BOYFRIEND for two years—my friends slipped away.

SENIOR, CHEMISTRY, JOHN CARROLL UNIVERSITY

I didn't meet enough upperclassmen when I was a freshman. I lived in the all-freshman dorm and had automatic friends, so I didn't branch out much until the second semester when I was involved in a play. I missed out on a lot of car trips that way!

SENIOR, BIOLOGY, OBERLIN COLLEGE

My biggest regret was not **joining my sorority** sooner. Those girls were my closest friends, and they made my schoolwork so much easier to do. College life as a whole was better just because they were there.

GRADUATE, ENVIRONMENTAL STUDIES, EMORY & HENRY COLLEGE

A CHANGE OF SCENERY

I transferred from one college to another. If I had to do it all over again, I would have just **stayed at the first school** and worked things out differently. The difference in the new school's curriculum was a big setback. Although all of my credits were transferred, it still took me longer to finish because I had to fulfill the school's requirements.

SENIOR, BIOCHEMISTRY, LEHMAN COLLEGE

My biggest regret is **not transferring out when I had the chance**. Although I have met a few wonderful people, I spent four years of my life in a place that I didn't like very much, where I did not fit in, and where there were very few people I could relate to. If you feel by mid-year of your freshman year that you made the wrong decision about which college to attend . . . leave! There's no sense in spending four years of your life being unhappy. It is a pain to fill out transfer applications, but do it on the chance that the next place will be better.

SENIOR, BIOLOGY, MILLSAPS COLLEGE

MISGUIDED ACTIONS

My biggest regret was **not going to class a lot** my freshman year. I thought that I didn't need to go to class since I didn't have to, so I usually didn't and I suffered the consequences!

SENIOR, PSYCHOLOGY/PRE-LAW, UNIVERSITY OF ILLINOIS—URBANA-CHAMPAIGN

As crappy as dorms may be, I regret NEVER HAVING HAD THE CHANCE to live in one, even if for one semester. You meet so many people in your building.

SENIOR, MICROBIOLOGY AND CELL SCIENCE, UNIVERSITY OF FLORIDA

I regret **not changing my major**. I thought I had to know what I wanted to do when I got to college, so I stuck with it even though I wasn't satisfied, because I was afraid of uncertainty.

SENIOR, GENDER STUDIES, NORTHWESTERN UNIVERSITY

My biggest regret from college was graduating. College is an amazing experience. Just try to enjoy each day, because the four years will fly by.

GRADUATE, POLITICAL SCIENCE, ST. JOSEPH'S UNIVERSITY

FINAL WORDS OF WISDOM

Now is your time to live.

SENIOR, ANTHROPOLOGY/INTERNATIONAL STUDIES,
NORTHWESTERN UNIVERSITY

INDULGE YOUR HEDONISTIC SIDE...

SPONTANEITY is the key to life. College is the last time you will have the freedom to ditch a Friday class to go snowboarding or skip your 12:40 to meet the boys down at the local pub for wings and beer. Take advantage.

GRADUATE, ANTHROPOLOGY/PRE-MEDICINE, ARIZONA STATE UNIVERSITY

You don't have to come out of college with a 4.0 GPA but it will get you a lot further in life than a 2.0. **Balance your time** accordingly.

GRADUATE, BIOLOGY, COLLEGE OF CHARLESTON

Don't be misled by **the crazy college life** you see in movies and on television. They only show the fun and not the consequences.

SENIOR, POLITICAL SCIENCE/CHINESE LANGUAGE, UNIVERSITY OF CALIFORNIA—IRVINE

Be open to **friendships with all different types of people.** It makes life much more interesting than hanging out with people just like you.

JUNIOR, BIOCHEMISTRY, UNIVERSITY OF CALIFORNIA—LOS ANGELES

Keep an open mind. Just because you've never done it, seen it, or tried it before doesn't make it bad.

GRADUATE, CRIMINAL JUSTICE/POLITICAL SCIENCE/HISTORY, INDIANA UNIVERSITY—BLOOMINGTON

Remember that **you have limits.** Don't overdo it.

GRADUATE, GOVERNMENT, DARTMOUTH COLLEGE

Go to class. It doesn't matter how hung-over you are, or if you haven't showered, or if you didn't do the work—go. You'll thank yourself later.

GRADUATE, LEGAL STUDIES, UNIVERSITY OF MASSACHUSETTS—AMHERST

Take the time to LISTEN; you'll learn more.

SENIOR, GOVERNMENT/SPANISH, UNIVERSITY OF TEXAS—AUSTIN

Buy a 24-hour planner. Trust me, it'll be the best $25 you spend each year.

JUNIOR, BIOLOGY AND NUCLEAR MEDICINE, UNIVERSITY OF THE INCARNATE WORD

Customize your education to something that you will enjoy. No one else will tell you how to make the best out of your education—you have to do that yourself!

GRADUATE, POLITICAL SCIENCE, UNIVERSITY OF CALIFORNIA—SAN DIEGO

Don't pretend to be something you're not. Don't do things just to fit in. Be yourself. There are countless others who will find you fun and exciting just for being YOU.

SENIOR, BIOLOGY/CHEMISTRY, DENISON UNIVERSITY

While in college you mature and grow outside the classroom far more than you grow inside the classroom. The relationships you make and the people you meet will be THE MEMORIES THAT YOU CARRY WITH YOU FOREVER. It's not how you studied for that big test, it's how you and your friends were able to drive to Atlantic City the night before the test and study on the way there and back and still do fine on the exam.

GRADUATE, BIOLOGY/NUTRITIONAL SCIENCES, PENNSYLVANIA STATE UNIVERSITY

FINAL WORDS OF WISDOM

Don't take yourself too seriously. If something seems like a huge failure, very urgent, or stressful, take a step back and look at how important that small event is compared to the whole picture. What seems incredibly important at the time usually isn't worth stressing yourself out about.

GRADUATE, BIOMEDICAL SCIENCES, MARQUETTE UNIVERSITY

I learned that **what you accomplish** doesn't create who you are, but who you are drives your accomplishments.

GRADUATE, ENGLISH AND MUSIC, COLLEGE OF WILLIAM & MARY

242

Act **confident** and you'll feel confident!

GRADUATE, PRE-MEDICINE, PENNSYLVANIA STATE UNIVERSITY

DEPEND ON YOURSELF. Even with the strongest support system, you still need to rely on Number One to get things done.

GRADUATE, PSYCHOLOGY, COLBY-SAWYER COLLEGE

Decisions you make for yourself, by yourself, make you the happiest.

GRADUATE, GOVERNMENT/GERMAN STUDIES, SMITH COLLEGE

LEARN YOUR LESSON

It's not so much WHAT you learn in college that helps you in life, it's **learning HOW to think** that will help you out in the long run. College doesn't teach you the solution to everything, but it teaches you how to come up with a solution on your own.

GRADUATE, BIOMETRY AND STATISTICS, CORNELL UNIVERSITY

I became **very humble** in college. I realized that there was actually very little about the world that I knew and have accepted that as a starting point to a post-college life of learning.

GRADUATE, ENGLISH, CORNELL UNIVERSITY

If you want to **follow your passions**, you will have to sacrifice a lot, but in the end you will be happier than the people who are just out for the money.

GRADUATE, BIOLOGY, GEORGETOWN UNIVERSITY

Don't cheat or take the easy road. You will have to struggle for most of the good things in life. WORK HARD and be proud of your work product.

GRADUATE, POLITICAL SCIENCE, UNIVERSITY OF CALIFORNIA—SAN DIEGO

I learned that HAVING A ROLE MODEL or mentor helps you get through the day.

GRADUATE, BIOLOGICAL SCIENCES, UNIVERSITY OF CALIFORNIA—DAVIS

Who you know is more important than what you know.

GRADUATE, BIOLOGY, INDIANA UNIVERSITY

Make the best of things and don't be a whiner. No matter how bad things look or how stressed out you are, things will work out one way or another. Things will work out the quickest if you keep your cool!

GRADUATE, INTERNATIONAL STUDIES, BRIGHAM YOUNG UNIVERSITY

Reinventing myself and finding new people to be friends with was the best part.

SENIOR, PSYCHOLOGY, UNIVERSITY OF SAN FRANCISCO

REBEL WITH A CAUSE

Take risks. Go out on a limb. Don't be afraid to do things you, your friends, and maybe even your family, don't think you're capable of. Put everything on the line, so you can **find out what you're really capable of** and who you really are.

SENIOR, PHILOSOPHY, ST. JOHN'S COLLEGE—ANNAPOLIS

It's important to take time and BE THE STEREOTYPE . . . dye your hair blue, be a pseudo-hippie, protest stuff . . . it'll never be as socially acceptable as it is now. . . .

GRADUATE, BIOCHEMISTRY AND CELL BIOLOGY, UNIVERSITY OF CALIFORNIA—SAN DIEGO

Cherish the time you have in college. Like our parents say, college is **the best time of your life**. It is very true.

GRADUATE, BIOLOGY, XAVIER UNIVERSITY

BE TRUE TO YOURSELF and live like there is no tomorrow.

SENIOR, PHILOSOPHY, COLLEGE OF WILLIAM & MARY

Find yourself. It'll be the most important thing you'll do.

SENIOR, PSYCHOLOGY, UNIVERSITY OF ILLINOIS—CHICAGO

You'll meet many different types of people in college. Take advantage of **the freedom to express who you are**, and learn from those who are different from you.

GRADUATE, ECONOMICS/COMMUNICATIONS, UNIVERSITY OF PENNSYLVANIA

College is the best place to approach new experiences since there are virtually no responsibilities compared to the "real world." Be sure to make that freedom worthwhile.

GRADUATE, PHYSIOLOGY/PSYCHOLOGY, UNIVERSITY OF MICHIGAN